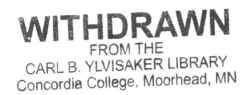

Praise for *Poetry and Prose Prompts*

"Future writers of poetry and prose must be led to the proposition that more than intellect is involved. Ken Rivenbark has written with convincing and persuasive insight into the challenge to the heart and soul, which is central to great writing."

—Mary Jane Caylor, Alabama State Board of Education

"Finally, hands-on, practical lessons to teach students how to write with style. Bravo! If teachers want a way to move students beyond the simple sentence to writing with style and expression, this book is your answer!"

—William McBride, national educational consultant;
author, *Entertaining an Elephant*

"Basic writing is one thing, writing with style in a variety of genres is another. Ken Rivenbark, drawing on his vast classroom experience, demonstrates specifically how teachers can help students achieve well beyond the NCTE standards."

—James L. Olivero, president, Staff Development Ltd.

JOSSEY-BASS TEACHER

Jossey-Bass Teacher provides K–12 teachers with essential knowledge and tools to create a positive and lifelong impact on student learning. Trusted and experienced educational mentors offer practical classroom-tested and theory-based teaching resources for improving teaching practice in a broad range of grade levels and subject areas. From one educator to another, we want to be your first source to make every day your best day in teaching. *Jossey-Bass Teacher* resources serve two types of informational needs—essential knowledge and essential tools.

Essential knowledge resources provide the foundation, strategies, and methods from which teachers may design curriculum and instruction to challenge and excite their students. Connecting theory to practice, essential knowledge books rely on a solid research base and time-tested methods, offering the best ideas and guidance from many of the most experienced and well-respected experts in the field.

Essential tools save teachers time and effort by offering proven, ready-to-use materials for in-class use. Our publications include activities, assessments, exercises, instruments, games, ready reference, and more. They enhance an entire course of study, a weekly lesson, or a daily plan. These essential tools provide insightful, practical, and comprehensive materials on topics that matter most to K–12 teachers.

Poetry and Prose Prompts

A Quick Guide for Teaching Writing Style

Ken Rivenbark

JOSSEY-BASS
A Wiley Imprint
www.josseybass.com

To my friend, my mentor, my dad

Published by Jossey-Bass

A Wiley Imprint

989 Market Street, San Francisco, CA 94103–1741   www.josseybass.com

Jossey-Bass books and products are available through most bookstores. To contact Jossey-Bass directly call our Customer Care Department within the U.S. at 800-956-7739, outside the U.S. at 317-572-3986, or fax 317-572-4002.

Jossey-Bass also publishes its books in a variety of electronic formats. Some content that appears in print may not be available in electronic books.

Library of Congress Cataloging-in-Publication Data

Rivenbark, Ken, date.
Poetry and prose prompts: a quick guide for teaching writing style /
Ken Rivenbark.—1st ed.
p. cm.
Includes bibliographical references and index.
ISBN-13: 978-0-7879-7879-2 (pbk.)
ISBN-10: 0-7879-7879-5 (pbk.)
1. English language—Composition and exercises—Study and teaching (Elementary) 2. English language—Style—Study and teaching (Elementary) 3. Creative writing (Elementary education) I. Title.
LB1576.R547 2006
372.62'3—dc22
2005032338
Printed in the United States of America

FIRST EDITION

PB Printing   10 9 8 7 6 5 4 3 2 1

ABOUT THIS BOOK

Writing is a fundamental and *essential* skill. It is taught early in our educational system, and it is a skill that serves us throughout our lives. Unfortunately, some students think that once they have learned the basics of grammar and spelling, they have nothing more to learn. As teachers, we must guide students to move beyond this stage and begin their journey of discovering their own personal styles.

There is a vast difference between writing and writing with *style*. Simple writing conveys information. Writing with style conveys not only overt information, but also "hidden" information, emotion, judgment, and intent. When you read something written with style and flair, you learn not only the information contained in the content of the writing, but you also learn something about the writer. And there is no question that writing with style has far more impact than simply writing to convey cold facts.

"Style" is a very personal characteristic, and everyone should certainly develop his or her own style of writing. But this places the teacher in a quandary. How can writing with style be taught?

An effective way of teaching and encouraging students to write with style is to explore the different styles of writing. As students discover the various traditional techniques of writing, they will begin to develop their own personal styles.

Students' writing styles are normally developed between grades 4 and 8. Most grade-4 students will have developed little if any of their own style of writing; their writing often tends to be to-the-point and informational, and they need to be shown the stylistic opportunities that await them. By grade 8, students should have begun to develop a unique style of writing, but this style frequently needs refinement and growth. So this book, used in different ways, serves the needs of students from grades 4 through 8.

The order of the material has been carefully chosen. We begin with an exploration of the different styles of poetry. Once students have become familiar with the distinctiveness and structure of poetry, they move on to characterization, learning to bring people to life through their writing. This naturally leads to narrative writing, where incidents can be so effectively described that the reader seems to be transported into the event itself.

Once they have completed the exercises and explorations in *Poetry and Prose Prompts: A Quick Guide for Teaching Writing Style,* students will better understand the power of the written word. More than that, they will recognize the importance of developing their own unique approach to writing . . . with style.

About the Author

Ken Rivenbark is a charismatic educator who speaks from the heart on issues that empower teachers. His personal opportunity to overcome a childhood processing disorder has led him to facilitate the teaching of writing in a visual manner that upper elementary and middle school students clearly understand.

Rivenbark is an experienced consultant who takes a hands-on approach with students and teachers as they grow together in their educational endeavors. He served as the director of curriculum development and instruction and as director of professional development for the online publisher Virtual Sage, in Fort Lauderdale, Florida. From 1999 to 2004 he was a lecturer with the University of North Carolina at Wilmington in the Watson School of Education, focusing on instructional design and language arts methods. He is a veteran classroom teacher of fifteen years, listed in *Who's Who Among America's Top Teachers* (1998 and 2005), and a certified writing trainer for the North Carolina Department of Public Instruction.

Acknowledgments

This book is the synthesis of an educational journey that has spanned more than twenty years. My career as an educator began in rural North Carolina and then traveled across the Atlantic to Europe, and back to the east coast of the United States. I hope that *Poetry and Prose Prompts* will serve as a tool to assist teachers in guiding students to merge the artistic power of writing into their everyday voice.

I thank the many educators who have taught me through the years by their active initiatives in the classroom. To my dear friends Gail Lucas, Chris Gentile, Carol Chase-Thomas, and Janet Slate-Rivenbark, who took their quest for educational excellence to the top of their field and inspired me along the way: each of you was instrumental in guiding this project from fantasy to reality.

I sincerely thank Steve Thompson, Angela Edwards, Virginia Wells, Jim Barber, and Tracy Cristal for their contributions of time and artistic expertise to the development of this book. And I thank as well the North Carolina Public School System, the Department of Defense Education Activity, and the Watson School of Education at the University of North Carolina at Wilmington for allowing me to grow and mature as an educator.

And finally, I thank all the students who have taught me to savor the moment, believe in miracles, and write from the heart.

CONTENTS

INTRODUCTION TO EXPRESSIVE WRITING

Expressive writing provides your students with numerous benefits to their educational growth.

- Expressive writing provides students with the opportunity to practice concise and precise word choices that create vivid images.
- Expressive writing provides students the opportunity to address various writing strategies that do not require lengthy assignments.
- Finally, expressive writing allows students to delve into their feelings, thoughts, and creativity.

Expressive writing promotes many of the *Standards for the English Language Arts,* as sponsored by the National Council of Teachers of English (NCTE) and International Reading Association (IRA). Specifically, in preparation for writing in various styles (haiku, diamonte, limericks, and so on), students must first read and become familiar with examples of those styles.

- Students read a wide range of print and nonprint texts to build an understanding of texts, of themselves, and of the cultures of the United States and the world; to acquire new information; to respond to the needs and demands of society and the workplace; and for personal fulfillment. Among these texts are fiction and nonfiction, classic and contemporary works.

The study of expressive writing spans ages and cultures. From the serenity of haiku to the gaiety of limericks, from Grecian fables to modern-day tall tales—the study of the styles of writing is the study of the people who wrote the material.

- Students read a wide range of literature from many periods in many genres to build an understanding of the many dimensions (for example, philosophical, ethical, aesthetic) of human experience. Poetry is especially helpful in strengthening students' vocabularies and their careful usage of words.
- Students apply a wide range of strategies to comprehend, interpret, evaluate, and appreciate texts. They draw on their prior experience, their interactions with other readers and writers, their knowledge of word meaning and of other texts, their

word identification strategies, and their understanding of textual features (for example, sound-letter correspondence, sentence structure, context, graphics). By comparing the different styles of writing, students learn how certain styles are more effective in different circumstances. Haiku, for example, conveys an appreciation of nature that limericks cannot.

• Students adjust their use of spoken, written, and visual language (for example, conventions, style, vocabulary) to communicate effectively with a variety of audiences and for different purposes.

• Students employ a wide range of strategies as they write and use different writing process elements appropriately to communicate with different audiences for a variety of purposes. Stylistic writing, such as poetry, emphasizes the importance of language structure and conventions. Diamonte, for example, emphasizes the difference between nouns, verbs, and adjectives in a way that prose cannot. And since some styles of writing require concise construction (such as haiku's seventeen syllables), close attention to spelling and grammar is essential.

• Students apply knowledge of language structure, language conventions (for example, spelling and punctuation), media techniques, figurative language, and genre to create, critique, and discuss print and nonprint texts. Some styles of writing, such as haiku and the tall tale, encourage and strengthen students' creative talents. Others, such as character and biographical sketches, require research on the subject.

• Students conduct research on issues and interests by generating ideas and questions and by posing problems. They gather, evaluate, and synthesize data from a variety of sources (for example, print and nonprint texts, artifacts, people) to communicate their discoveries in ways that suit their purpose and audience. In perhaps the greatest achievement of learning to write with style, students become aware that expressive writing is both useful and enjoyable.

• Students use spoken, written, and visual language to accomplish their own purposes (for example, for learning, enjoyment, persuasion, and the exchange of information).

Teacher Support for Facilitating Expressive Writing

The expressive writing exercises in this book are designed to accomplish a variety of objectives. They help students build composition skills in a variety of forms. Working in the specific forms can help provide students with the confidence and flexibility they need for writing well in all forms. These skills will serve students well, from writing college applications to writing notes to family members.

They teach topic-selection skills: a student learns that the best topic for a haiku is different from the best topic for a personal essay. They also provide a painless way to understand a wide variety of literary genres.

The exercises are beneficial to the teacher as well. They offer you the opportunity to teach planning and judgment skills—in effect, editing and self-editing skills. And they have the potential for you to encourage students to appreciate reading, as well as to foster writing skills.

How will students benefit from learning to write expressively? They will demonstrate appropriate language usage, spelling, mechanics, and other conventions of English in speaking and writing. They will learn to read orally with fluency and expression.

They will recognize and respond to different types of literature, such as fantasy, reality, poetry, nursery rhymes, drama, and song. And of course, students will strengthen their skills in writing on directed topics.

What will students be accomplishing through this course in expressive writing? Students will compose various fiction, nonfiction, poetry, and drama using both self-selected and assigned topics and forms (for example, personal and imaginative narratives, research reports, diaries, journals, logs, rules, personal and business letters, or instructions).

They will plan and make judgments about what to include in written products (such as narratives of personal experiences, creative stories, or skits based on familiar stories or experiences).

Finally, they will study the characteristics of literary genres (fiction, nonfiction, drama, and poetry) through reading a variety of literature and other text (such as young adult novels, short stories, biographies, plays, free verse, or narrative poems) and evaluating what impact genre-specific characteristics have on the meaning of the text.

Lesson plans have been provided for each of the writing styles in this book. However, you may also incorporate expressive writing into your existing lesson plans. You can do this in a variety of ways.

You can establish a periodic expressive writing lesson to reinforce learning objectives keyed to reading lessons. Conversely, you can introduce reading lessons through the expressive writing lessons in order to stimulate students' interest in the form.

You can assign individual extra credit for expressive writing projects or assign expressive writing as a component of group research projects for end-of-unit review. You can introduce segments of the lessons during the beginning or end of class periods to provide enrichment to existing lessons throughout the week, or you can use these lessons as transition lessons. (This can be especially useful before or after holidays when students are active and/or restless.)

One of the advantages of these expressive writing lessons is their flexibility in scheduling and time requirements. Most lessons require between 30 and 45 minutes to complete; however, you can also incorporate single segments of these lessons into existing lessons.

Alternatively, you may want to introduce the lessons over a series of days, refreshing students' memories with each new step. For your planning and scheduling, each segment of a lesson includes an approximate time. (Of course, this can vary considerably, depending on specific circumstances, and should only be used as a guide.)

It is quite normal for students to approach expressive writing with reluctance. This reluctance can be overcome in a variety of ways.

You can begin with a class brainstorming session, demonstrating that expressive writing can be fun and relaxed. You can introduce silly versions of many forms, such as cat and dog haiku, to show that expressive writing can be fun.

Activities include introducing a topic and a beginning sentence for narratives and having each member of the class add to the last member's sentence, as the story develops spontaneously. You can ask the class to generate a list of their own writing prompts.

As you focus on the different styles of poetry and prose, ask students questions keyed to the specific expressive writing form being considered, and list their responses. Students can use those to draw on ideas for writing.

Most of all, you should emphasize the idea that, while writers may change direction when writing, there are no "mistakes." There is only writing that can be improved on.

Whichever topic is being considered, you should always encourage exploration and experimentation. Your feedback should be either positive verbal recognition or positive written recognition of student efforts—but it should consistently be positive. The lessons will be most effective if students receive teacher comments and encouragement and full credit for their accomplishments.

PART ONE

INTRODUCTION TO POETRY

Students discover some of the most powerful forms of expressive writing in poetry. Because poetry tends to be highly structured and concise, with each individual word carefully chosen and used, students sometimes regard writing poetry as difficult work to be avoided.

Try presenting the challenges of writing poetry as puzzles to be solved, rather than as work to be done. And turn the conciseness of poetry to your advantage. A complete poem may be written in just a few dozen words, giving your students the satisfaction of achievement in a relatively short amount of time.

When many people think of "poetry," they think of writing that rhymes. Consequently, arguably the most enjoyable challenge for students to tackle is that of finding words that rhyme. (How many words rhyme with "tree"? What rhymes with "orange"? What rhymes with "rhyme"?) Once students become adept at thinking of words that rhyme, they can move on to the challenges of cadence and syllable count.

When students become comfortable with the structure of poetry, they are ready to tackle the meaning behind the words themselves. Emphasize to students that since they don't have the flexibility of inserting a word or sentence wherever they need it (as they can do in prose), they must carefully choose just the right words to convey the specific meaning (or, quite possibly, several meanings) that they desire.

Writing a message where each word is carefully chosen for its meaning, its implications, its relationship to the other words around it, and its sound when pronounced— now that's a challenge! But properly presented, it's a challenge that your students will embrace with enthusiasm.

Students may question the relevancy of writing poetry in today's modern world. This is normal; students are constantly reading prose, both in and out of school, but generally have little exposure to poetry. So students may well ask why writing poetry is important to them.

Writing poetry builds a specific set of language skills. Poetic forms often require a specific number of syllables per verse. Writing in a strict syllabic style gives students practice in choosing the best words to fit within a confined space, frequently resulting in a greater understanding and appreciation of word structure and effect. Because many poems are confined to a certain number of lines (four for quatrains) or syllables (haiku), writers must select their words with precision.

Chosen words must make sense in context, have an appealing sound (alliteration and onomatopoeia can be introduced), and fit within the rhyme scheme, meter, or line specifications. This helps students develop concise word skills and learn to write within specifications. This is a practical exercise because most writers have to meet word limits when writing. In addition, the practice with words further develops students' verbal skills. This is a concrete set of skills that can transfer to better reading and writing skills.

Finally, because poetry is a highly individualized form of writing that lends itself to personal exploration, these early lessons introduce students to a form of creative self-expression. As such, learning to write within these forms contributes to students' growth and development as individuals.

However, listing the benefits of writing poetry will not win over many students. Their first reaction might be negative because poetry is perceived as unfamiliar or not a part of our popular culture. You can remind students that song lyrics are a form of poetry: lyric poetry. In addition, teachers can refer to students' early introduction to reading through nonsense verses such as those of Dr. Seuss.

You can ask students to bring in lyrics or verse they like, followed with a discussion on why such verses are poetry. (You should ensure that your students' lyrics are topic- and age-appropriate before they share them with their classmates.) You can also share with students their own favorite verses, especially if they are funny or otherwise appealing to the grade level. For example, ballads can be introduced with Edward Lear's "The Owl and the Pussycat" or W. S. Gilbert's "The Yarn of the Nancy Belle." For haiku, you can easily find popular cat and dog haiku on the Internet. Students generally enjoy such verse.

The following lessons introduce five forms of poetry to students: *haiku, diamonte, quatrains, limericks,* and *ballads.* These forms were selected because:

1. They are typically short, thus accessible to student writing in the classroom setting;

2. They are specific in rhyme scheme, meter, or other requirements, so they introduce students to the requirements of disciplined verse; and

3. They lend themselves to experimentation, so they are fun for student writers.

Demonstrating that poetry can be enjoyable and can also be applied to students' daily experience will ease student concerns about writing poetry. Most readers enjoy the rhythm of poetry, and poetry is an accessible form of literature. Poetry is a complex, imaginative form that young writers can explore and enjoy.

HAIKU

The haiku is a unique form of poetry with Japanese origins. The poetry structure is clear and concise with a focus on simple, sensory images using nature as its theme. The haiku scaffolding consists of three lines using five, seven, and five syllables, respectively.

Essential Elements

The essential elements of a haiku make it easily recognizable. A haiku

- Is a poem form originating from Japan that contains vivid words and phrases to describe nature
- Communicates thoughts and/or feelings
- Consists of seventeen unrhymed syllables organized in three lines—five syllables in the first line, seven in the next, and five in the last line

Standards Haiku Support

Haiku poetry supports a number of the NCTE/IRA standards, as noted in the Introduction to Expressive Writing.

As they learn about haiku, students will strengthen their vocabularies by developing a list of specific descriptive nature words and by learning how to use them poetically. Students will also learn the importance of counting syllables, which provides an introduction to poetic meter. Finally, students will begin learning how to create meaning within a controlled writing form. This provides a good introduction to studying other forms of poetry.

Lesson Plan Example: Haiku

Activity Objectives

In this lesson, students will

- Strengthen their vocabularies by developing a list of specific descriptive nature words
- Use descriptive vocabulary poetically
- Recognize the importance of the syllable in poetic structure
- Write descriptively within a controlled writing form

Activity Summary

The students will first become familiar with the structure of haiku poetry. Then they will examine a picture or photograph of a nature scene and develop a list of descriptive words that express their feelings about the scene. The next step is to use those descriptive words to develop a haiku poem as a group. Finally, each student will develop his or her own haiku, based on a different nature picture. At the conclusion, the students share their haiku poems with each other.

Materials

- Samples of haiku poetry from children (Choose several from the examples found at the end of this lesson, or search the Internet for "haiku.") For small groups, these may be printed (using a large font for easy reading) on 8½ by 11-inch paper; for larger groups, they may be written on poster board or on flip-chart pages.
- A writing surface (such as a flip chart, whiteboard, or chalkboard) for developing haiku as a group
- A display surface for displaying pictures (The writing surface may be appropriate.) If no display surface is available, the teacher may simply show the pictures individually or pass them around to the members of the group.
- Pictures of nature scenes cut from magazines (Old *National Geographic* magazines are excellent sources of pictures.) The pictures can be pre-selected by the teacher, or the class can find their own pictures as a separate preceding activity.

Description of Activity

1. Statement of Objectives
   - Tell the students, "Today, we are going to work together as a group to write some haiku poetry. First, I will show you some examples of haiku, and then we will do one together. Then we will look at some pictures to come up with some ideas so that you can write your own haiku. We will also discuss the descriptive words that you will be using to write your haiku. When you are finished, we will discuss your poems within our group."

2. Class Discussion

- Gather the students around the writing surface so that everyone can see the haiku being developed. Ask whether anyone can tell you what a haiku is. If no one responds, explain that a haiku is a form of poetry popular in Japan.

- Tell the group an overall description of a haiku. "A haiku is a short poem that contains vivid words and phrases that describe something you've seen in nature. Haiku can also express your thoughts and feelings about what you have seen. They don't have to rhyme."

- Now describe the specific characteristics of a haiku. "A haiku consists of only three lines and seventeen syllables. The first line has five syllables, line two has seven syllables, and line three has five syllables." Write the sequence on the display surface so you can refer to it. An easy way to count the syllables is to have the students lightly clap or tap out the syllables in each line.

- Show the class an example of a haiku. Have them read it aloud, counting the syllables in each line. (Younger students may enjoy clapping the rhythm of the poem, one clap for each syllable.) Show the students how each line contributes to the theme of the poem.

- Since some students may assume that all poetry must follow some sort of rhyming pattern, point out to them that haiku poems do not need to rhyme. However, they do have a specific structure of three lines with seventeen syllables.

- Show the class several additional haiku examples, discussing both the syllable count and the theme of the poem, until the group has a good understanding of how a haiku should be written.

3. Group Activity

- Display one of the pictures of a nature scene and ask the students to consider it. "Think about the nature scene in this picture. What do you notice? What descriptive words can you use to describe the scene?" Write the descriptive words on the display surface as students suggest them. After you have listed some words that relate to the picture, tell the students that they will now develop a haiku about that particular scene.

- Ask whether someone can develop the first line of the haiku. Write the proposed line on the writable surface for the entire group to see. Check whether it meets the requirements of a haiku. (Specifically, does it have five syllables? Does it describe the nature scene or the feelings evoked by the scene?) If the students have a difficult time in determining the correct number of syllables, suggest that they clap once for each syllable as they read the line. If the line does not have the correct number of syllables, work as a group on improving the line until it meets the specifications of a haiku.

- Once the group has developed a five-syllable opening line, ask them for suggestions for the second line (seven syllables) and then the third (five syllables). Write all suggestions so the entire group can see them. If you have several suggestions for the lines, have the group pick their favorite first, second, and third lines.

- Display the finished haiku so everyone can see it, along with the scene it describes. If time permits, repeat this exercise until students develop confidence in writing haiku.

4. Independent Activity

- For their own haiku, let the students use the pictures that the class looked at earlier. Have each student select one picture that he or she likes.

- Tell the students, "Now that we have practiced together, you are going to write your own haiku, using the nature scene that you have chosen. If you need help with any of the description words, or if you have trouble with the syllable count, raise your hand and I will help you."

- After they are finished, have them share their haiku with the group.

5. Closure

- When everyone has finished, ask the students whether they enjoyed writing haiku. For review, ask what they remember about haiku. "Who can tell me what a haiku is? How many syllables do the lines have? What kind of words and phrases do you need? How many lines are there in a haiku? How many syllables are in each line?"

- Thank the students for sharing their poems and ask whether they have any questions about writing haiku.

Poetry Examples: **Haiku**

These are some haiku written by students. Students often need examples to study before they feel confident in developing their own haiku, and these haiku will serve as illustrations in the lesson's activities.

Rainstorm

Raindrops falling down
Harder and harder they fall
Sun is soon to come

Fall

Leaves changing colors
Wind rustles the leaves of trees
To the ground they fall

Summer

Sunny days are here
No responsibility
Lie on beach all day

Thunderstorm

Raindrops falling hard
Lightning brighter than a star
Thunder gets louder

River

Down at the river
Sitting alone, by myself
Water speaks to me.

Jump, Jump, Jump! It calls.
Won't you come and play with me?
Will you be my friend?

Gardens

Gardens life teaming
Colors, greenery, flowers
Its pleasures and joys.

Snow

Snow ever falling
On car and I sixty-four
Will we make it there?

Ocean

Always inviting
Tide and time wait for no man
Always merciless

Summer

Sunshine in the sky
Thunderstorms to come later
The weather changes

Colors

Beautiful colors
Painted in the sky for me
Show me God is near

Bountiful colors
Stay right here, don't go away.
Thank you for the show.

DIAMONTE

Diamonte poetry is constructed of seven lines of vivid descriptions that contrast two opposite nouns or subjects.

Essential Elements

The essential elements of diamonte poetry are usually appreciated by students because their visual nature makes them easy to see and understand. A diamonte poem

- Focuses on two opposite or contrasting subjects
- Is arranged in seven lines whose lengths form a diamond pattern (that is, the first and last lines are the shortest and the middle line is the longest)

A diamonte poem is composed of sixteen words that are arranged in the following format:

Line 1: one noun

Line 2: two adjectives describing line 1

Line 3: three participles, or "-ing words," describing line 1

Line 4: four nouns, the first two relating to line 1 and the second two relating to line 7

Line 5: three participles, or "-ing words," describing line 7

Line 6: two adjectives describing line 7

Line 7: one noun that is the opposite of line 1

Standards Diamonte Support

Diamonte supports a number of the NCTE/IRA standards, as noted in the Introduction to Expressive Writing.

Writing a diamonte teaches students to observe the comparative qualities in two subjects. In addition, it allows them to understand the importance of word length in poetic structure. It also instructs them that writing can have a visual element. Writing with a visual element can transfer to a later understanding of effective web-related text. Finally, students learn to recognize the importance of the length of words in building a poetic structure and to see the commonalities in two "opposite" subjects.

Lesson Plan Example: Diamonte

Activity Objectives

In this lesson, students will

- Use planning strategies (such as brainstorming, mapping, webbing, reading, or discussion) to generate topics and organize ideas
- Consider the commonalities in two "opposite" subjects
- Explore the visual element of writing poetry

Activity Summary

Students will first learn the structure of diamonte poetry, both the relative line lengths and the types of words that are used on each line of the poem. The students will explore the concept of contrasting topics and then use one of the contrasting pairs as a basis for a group-developed diamonte. Finally, the students will individually develop their own diamontes and then share their projects with the group.

Materials
- Several samples of diamonte poetry on a medium easily viewed by the group (such as transparency, flip chart, or poster board), taken from the examples from the end of this session
- A writing surface that is easily seen by entire group (such as a whiteboard or flip chart)

Description of Activity
1. Statement of Objectives
   - "Now we are going to learn about another form of expressive writing, a poem called a diamonte. Does anyone know what a diamonte is? Does diamonte sound like another word that is familiar to you?" Guide them to guessing *diamond*. "Based on that, can you guess what a diamonte poem might be?" Consider the different responses and then tell the students, "We are going to learn what makes a diamonte poem different from other poems, and then you will create your own diamonte."
2. Class Discussion
   - "A diamonte focuses on two opposite or contrasting subjects such as *playing* versus *working*. It is arranged in seven lines that form a diamond pattern." Show your students one of the sample diamonte. If possible, draw a "diamond" (sparkle included!) around the diamonte to emphasize the point about shape in this form.

- Following the guidelines in the essential elements at the beginning of this section, the first line of a diamonte is a single word, the second line has two words, the third line has three words, and the fourth line has four words. Count off the words on the sample diamonte as you define its structure.

- "From that point, the lines decrease in length. The fifth line has three words. The sixth line has only two words. And the bottom line, line 7, has a single word."

- Explain that a diamonte not only has a well-defined shape, but it also has rules about the makeup of each line of the poem. "Lines 1 and 7 are your contrasting subjects. Line 2 contains two adjectives that describe the subject in line 1, and line 6 contains two adjectives that describe the subject in line 7." Point out these words on the sample diamonte.

- "Line 3 will be three verbs that end with '-ing' that are about the topic in line 1, and line 5 is made up of three '-ing' verbs that are about the topic in line 7." Again, point to the appropriate words in the poem.

- "Finally, line 4 is the line where the two subjects meet. Line four contains four words—the first two words are two nouns about the subject in line 1, and the remaining two words of the line are two nouns about the subject in line 7." Emphasize the difference between the two words that start the line and the two words that end it.

- Point out to the group that, like the haiku previously discussed, the diamonte does not need to follow a rhyming pattern.

3. Group Activity

- Brainstorm with the students and come up with some contrasting subjects, such as *school* and *home, adult* and *child, ocean* and *desert, day* and *night, dog* and *cat,* or *spring* and *fall.*

- Then pick one of the suggested subject pairs and work as a group in developing a list of adjectives, a number of verbs that end with -ing, and a variety of nouns—all of which are associated with the two subjects.

- Using those word lists, have the group develop a diamonte and write it on the board or flip chart. (If possible, go around the group and have each student suggest one word for the diamonte.)

4. Individual Activity

- Have each student choose a pair of contrasting subjects. Help any students who cannot decide on a pair of opposites. "Now, I want you to work on your own diamonte. If anyone needs assistance, raise your hand. When everyone is finished, we will share with each other."

- After they are finished writing their diamonte, have them share their poems with the group.

5. Closure

- Ask the students for the characteristics of a diamonte. Then summarize the lesson. "A diamonte is a poem with contrasting subjects, written with seven lines whose lengths form a diamond pattern."

Poetry Examples: **Diamonte**

Here are some diamonte written by students. You can use them as examples in performing the class activities.

Summer
Hot humid
Swimming sweating playing
Beach sunshine coats snowman
Sledding sneezing snowing
Cold icy
Winter

Dog
Smelly friendly
Loving barking wagging
Hound puppy Siamese kitten
Napping chasing purring
Stubborn soft
Cat

Dog
Happy loyal
Barking chasing loving
Friend protect scratch nap
Purring chasing exploring
Finicky snooty
Cat

Beach
Hot sandy
Swimming relaxing walking
Shells ocean trees streams
Hiking camping fishing
Cool rocky
Mountains

Cats
Playful glamorous
Scratching meowing climbing
Kitten claws aquarium fins
Swimming darting splashing
Slimy scaly
Fish

Land
Brown green
Blowing growing sowing
Mountains plains mammals fish
Flowing ebbing drifting
Blue turquoise
Sea

Surfing
Active enjoyable
Swimming carving paddling
Water spray leap slide
Scraping flipping spinning
Difficult painful
Skating

Country
Quiet fragrant
Riding growing living
Barns tractors skyscrapers taxis
Working hurrying hiding
Noisy busy
City

QUATRAINS

The word *quatrain* comes from Latin and French words meaning "four." The quatrain is a poem or stanza of four lines. It is a popular form of poetry that can be written about any type of subject and can be silly or serious. Quatrains may or may not rhyme. Famous poets like William Blake and T. S. Eliot often used quatrains.

Essential Elements

The essential elements of quatrains are rather simple. A quatrain

- Is a four-line poem in which each line has a strong rhythm and similar syllable count
- Can be written about any subject, so it can be either silly or serious
- Can have a variety of rhyming patterns (such as AAAA, ABAB, ABCB, AABB) or does not need to rhyme at all

Standards Quatrains Support

The study of quatrains supports a number of the NCTE/IRA standards, as noted in the Introduction to Expressive Writing. In learning about quatrains, students become more aware of the word rhythms and the effect rhythm has on readers. It also gives them further practice with word syllables. Learning about quatrains also reinforces the lesson learned in haiku that verse does not have to rhyme in order to be poetry.

Lesson Plan Example: Quatrains

Activity Objectives

In this session, students will

- Use planning strategies (such as brainstorming, mapping, webbing, reading, or discussion) to generate topics and organize ideas

- Learn to recognize and identify syllabic cadence
- Write their own material with a defined syllabic cadence

Activity Summary

Students will listen to poetry with strong syllabic cadence. When they are comfortable with identifying the cadence of a poem, students will write their own lines, following a predefined cadence.

Materials

- Some examples of quatrains prewritten on a medium that is easily seen by the group, such as flip-chart pages or poster board (Some examples of quatrains written by students are found at the end of this lesson.)
- A dry erase board or other surface that can be written on and viewed by the entire group

Description of Activities

1. Statement of Objectives
   - Display several sample quatrains for the students. "This type of poem is called a 'quatrain.' Can anyone guess where the name comes from?" If necessary, suggest similar words such as *quarter* or *quartet* until the students can guess what the word *quatrain* is describing (a four-line poem). "Today we will work together on studying quatrains. By the end of this lesson, you will know how to write your own quatrains."

2. Class Discussion
   - Select a quatrain from the samples that follow this lesson and display it so everyone in the group can see it. "Here's a quatrain. Let's read it together." After reading the poem, tell the group what makes a quatrain different from other poems. "A quatrain is a four-line poem. Different lines can rhyme with each other, but they don't have to."
   - "But a quatrain is not just any four lines. Lines of a quatrain poem have a similar *cadence*." Read the lines of the quatrain again, putting heavy emphasis on the poem's rhythm. For example

   He *growls* and he's *fur*ry,

   He *makes* me quite *hur*ry.

   not only rhymes (which students usually pick up on quickly), but follows a weak-*strong*-weak-weak-*strong*-weak cadence. Cadence is typically more difficult for students to grasp; repeated readings (aloud) of several sample quatrains can be helpful.

- "Now let's try writing a quatrain as a group." Show an example of the first line or two of a sample quatrain. "I'll give you the start of a quatrain. What would the rest of the quatrain look like?" Students, as a group, will complete the quatrain and discuss the reasons for the lines they chose.

3. Group Activity

   - "Now let's try to develop a whole quatrain of our own. Who can suggest the first line of our quatrain?" Have students assist you with creating a quatrain, emphasizing appropriate word rhythm and syllable count.

4. Individual Activity

   - Assign students to write a quatrain of their own. (Older students should work individually; younger students may work better in pairs.) "Now write your own quatrain. If you need help, raise your hand. When everyone is ready, we will share our quatrains."

5. Closure

   - Ask the students to share their quatrains and show how they used strong rhythm in writing their quatrains.

   - Ask students, "What are the key ingredients of a quatrain?" (Strong rhythm and similar syllable count)

Poetry Examples: **Quatrains**

These quatrains were written by students. They can be used as examples in guiding students in their study of quatrains.

Birds are so lucky 'cause they can fly,
Soaring through the air, so free and high,
Able to cruise wherever they like
And poop on those that may pass by.

Jon's big dog Rover
Won't let me come over;
He growls and he's furry,
He makes me quite hurry.

If you send a poem to me,
I'll send one back to you.
We'll read each other's poems
And know our love is true.

I love to talk.
I love to walk.
But most of all
I love to rhyme.

Ice cream is my favorite food.
Let me tell you why.
It puts me in the greatest mood.
I never want to cry.

Esmeralda danced 'til dawn,
Her happiness displaying,
A taste for none, a bite for all,
Echoed in her laughter's call.

My pony's name is Buttercup,
I won her in a raffle.
I like to tell her of my woe,
But her answer is a baffle!

Butterflies are graceful.
Fluttering from place to place.
Watching them in motion
Puts a big smile on my face.

LIMERICKS

A limerick is a five-line poem written with one *couplet* and one *triplet.* Just as a couplet is a two-line rhymed poem, a triplet is a three-line rhymed poem. Some people say that the limerick was invented by soldiers returning from France to the Irish town of Limerick in the 1700s.

Essential Elements

Of all the poetic forms, the limerick is arguably the one that students like the best. Many students are already familiar with limericks, and they enjoy their humorous content. But many students do not recognize the essential elements of limericks. A limerick

- Is a light, humorous verse composed of five lines
- Contains three eight- or nine-syllable lines (the first, second, and fifth) that rhyme
- Contains two five- or six-syllable lines (the third and fourth) that rhyme with each other

Standards Limericks Support

The study of limericks supports a number of the NCTE/IRA standards, as noted in the Introduction to Expressive Writing.

Students will explore the structure and rhyming patterns that are specific to limericks. Perhaps even more importantly, students will discover that verse can be light and humorous—both fun to write and fun to read.

Lesson Plan Example: Limericks

Activity Objectives

In this lesson, students will

- Recognize the strong syllabic cadence that define limerick structure
- Understand the importance of rhyming words and their placement within the limerick
- Write their own limericks

Activity Summary

The students will understand the characteristics of limerick poetry and how limericks differ from other forms of poetry. They will examine several limericks, and then the group will write a limerick themselves. Finally, each student will develop his or her own limerick.

Materials

- Some sample limericks (see the end of this lesson) on a display surface easily seen by the group, such as a flip chart, poster board, or overhead transparency
- A surface to write on, such as a whiteboard or a flip chart, for the group's writing of a limerick

Description of Activities

1. Statement of Objectives

   - "Today we are going to study a form of poetry known as a limerick. You may have already read or heard limericks. By the end of the lesson, you will be able to write your own limericks."

2. Class Discussion

   - Ask whether your students remember the theme of subject matter of haiku poetry. (Nature) Now show them several examples of limericks and ask them whether they can guess what the theme or subject of limericks is typically. (Humor)

   - Select a limerick and display it for the students to see. "Let's read this limerick aloud together. Then we'll look at all of the essential elements required in a limerick."

   - "A limerick is a light, humorous verse composed of five lines." Emphasize the five lines in the displayed limerick. "It contains three eight- or nine-syllable lines that rhyme." Point to them. "And it contains two five-syllable lines that rhyme with each other." Point to the pair of rhyming lines.

- "A limerick also has a strong cadence. Cadence is formed from the pattern that develops between syllables that are emphasized and syllables that are not. Listen to this line, and notice its cadence." Read one line of the limerick, placing extra weight on the emphasized syllables. "Limericks typically follow a 'strong-weak-weak' cadence, although a line can begin or end with one or two weak syllables." Read the same line, pointing out the strong-weak-weak cadence. Now read the entire limerick, showing how the strong-weak-weak cadence is followed throughout the limerick.

- "Many limericks traditionally begin with 'There once was a [thing] from a [place],' where you supply your own words for the thing and the place." Show students the cadence in "There *once* was a ***thing*** from a *place*." "Although you don't have to begin your limericks this way, it's an easy way to tell your reader or audience that you have written a limerick."

3. Group Activity

- "Now, let's work together as a class to create a limerick. First, let's develop a list of words that rhyme." Suggest a word, and have the students suggest other words that rhyme with it. Then do the same for a second word.

- "Next, let's brainstorm, and call out ideas of what the poem could be about." Write the best ideas on the board, and then have the students choose their favorite subject.

- "Finally, let's work together using the ideas that we came up with in order to write the limerick. Let's write the first line." Have the group develop the first line of the limerick, ending with one of the rhyming words from the first list. Try to approach the traditional limerick cadence, but anything close is acceptable.

- "Now let's write the second line." Have the group develop another line of the limerick. It should be approximately nine syllables in length, and it should rhyme with the first line. Proper cadence is desirable, but not essential.

- "Now let's write the third line." Have the group develop the third line of the limerick. This line should be shorter than the first two lines, approximately five syllables in length, and it should end with one of the rhyming words from the second list. As before, proper cadence is not essential.

- "We're almost done. Now let's write the fourth line." Have the group develop the fourth line of the limerick. It should match the third line in syllable count and rhyme.

- "Now let's finish our limerick by writing the last line." Have the group develop the fifth line. It should match the first and second lines in syllable count and rhyme.

- "Now let's read the entire limerick and see what we've accomplished." Read the limerick to the students, or have the students read it aloud as a group. "Congratulations! You've written a limerick."

- If time permits, note the emphasized syllables in the limerick and see whether it follows the traditional limerick cadence. Have the group see whether they can improve the limerick's cadence by substituting or rearranging words in the lines with improper cadence.

4. Individual Activity

- "Now use the ideas given on the board, as well as a dictionary and the-saurus, to create your own limerick. It should be appropriate, be humorous, and include all the essential elements. If you finish early, illus-trate your limerick on a separate sheet of paper. If you have questions, raise your hand."

5. Closure

- "Let's end our session by reading some of your limericks out loud. If you illustrated your limerick, please show the class. Remember that today we focused on and composed a style of poetry known as a limerick."

Poetry Examples: **Limericks**

Here are some limericks written by students. Although the cadence is rough in places, they follow the limerick requirements of AABBA rhyming as well as the length of each line (long, long, short, short, long).

If your students are up to the challenge, point out to them the cadence that a limerick typically follows (*strong*, weak, weak, with one or two weak syllables at the beginning and end of each line), and see whether they can improve the cadence of the limericks supplied here.

There once was a fish named Miguel.
His tank made him feel very well.
He'd always get fed.
No tears he would shed.
Life to him was so simple and swell.

There once was a puppy named Max.
His eyes were blind from cataracts.
He'd bump into doors
And get lots of sores.
He now has to sniff his own tracks.

There once was a man from Nantucket
Who blew his nose in a bucket.
He stored it in jars
And used it on cars.
Don't ask why—he'll make you suck it.

There once was a lady named Ruth
Who lived in a telephone booth.
She opened the door.
Fell down on the floor.
And now she is missing a tooth.

There once was a student named Scott
Whose homework he always forgot,
His teacher turned red,
His mom said you're dead,
But none of that helped him a lot.

There once was a girl named Ellie.
She liked to shoot her Benelli.
She would fill a deer
With dread and with fear.
Then go and dine at the deli.

There once was a mouse named Thumper.
He ate until he was plumper.
Gum, soda, and chips
Made him lick his lips.
He'd sleep all day on a bumper.

I have a hat I like the best.
I found it when shopping out west.
It has a feather
Made out of leather.
I found it in a leather bird nest.

There once was a girl named Jeanine
Who jumped on a big trampoline.
She bounced very high.
Up into the sky
And soared like a wild peregrine.

There once was an old man named Chuck
Who seemed cursed and full of bad luck.
He was hit in the head—
Surely, he should be dead
Since he was hit by an old truck.

BALLADS

A ballad is a story that follows a verse format that has a sing-song flavor. In fact, students can easily compare the structure of a ballad with that of a song that uses the verse-chorus format.

Essential Elements

A ballad

- Is a story written in verse format
- Contains strong characters and vivid and dramatic action
- Is written in stanzas that have a strong rhythm but don't necessarily rhyme
- Has a two-line rhyming refrain that reflects an important element of the story
- Captures the emotion of the events as it tells the story

Standards Ballads Support

The study of ballads supports many of the NCTE/IRA standards, as noted in the Introduction to Expressive Writing.

Ballads combine narrative and poetic forms, so they provide a good transition lesson between poetry and learning to write narratives. In ballads, characterization, which is the focus of the next unit, becomes important. When putting a story into ballad form, students learn to maintain plot structure while eliminating unnecessary words.

In addition, in developing refrains to point out the key point of a story, they understand the importance of key, or thesis, statements to maintain readers' understanding and interest.

Lesson Plan Example: Ballads

Activity Objectives

In this lesson, students will

- Understand the essential elements of ballads
- Recognize the importance of the refrain in linking the ballad together

- See how the stanzas move the story along
- Write a ballad on a subject of their choice

Activity Summary

The students will become familiar with the structure, purpose, and essential elements of a ballad by examining a prewritten ballad. The students will then, as a group exercise, write a short ballad of their own. If time and circumstances permit, individual students may be assigned to write their own ballads.

Materials

- Overhead projector
- Examples of ballads (see end of this lesson for several samples written by students; you can also search the Internet to find a variety of ballads and folk lyrics)
- Transparency of the pre-writing form

Description of Activities

1. Statement of Objectives
   - "In class today we will explore writing ballads. By the end of this lesson, you will know how to write your own ballads using the essential elements."

2. Class Discussion
   - Have the students read several examples of ballads, and then ask students to describe a ballad and the possible steps to writing one. "What characteristics do these ballads have in common?"
   - Guide the discussion so that students understand that a ballad:

     Is a verse that tells a story

     Contains strong characters and vivid and dramatic action

     Is written in stanzas that have a strong rhythm but don't necessarily rhyme

     Has a two-line rhyming refrain that reflects an important element of the story

     Captures the emotion of the events as it tells the story in verse
   - Show the students the ballad pre-writing exercise (found at the end of this lesson). Show them how to use it to develop a ballad from the overall topic to the repeated refrain, and finally to the sequence of the stanzas that tell the story.

3. Group Activity
   - Lead the students in writing a ballad on a blank overhead transparency. "We'll write a ballad together. First, let's brainstorm possible topics for ballads." Topics might include local sports figures or an event happening in school that students find interesting.

- "What is a good refrain, or repeated line, for this topic?" Write suggestions on the board, and then have the group choose their favorite.

- "What do we want to have happen in the first stanza?" When the students have decided what they want to say in the first stanza, tell them, "Now let's write the first stanza together." Ask them for suggestions for writing the first line, then the second, then the others. If multiple suggestions are made, have the students pick their favorite.

- Repeat the process for the remaining stanzas. Guide the students into bringing the ballad to a logical close and an emotional climax.

- "You have now written your first ballad."

4. Individual Activity

- "Now, you will write your own ballad. Just as we did as a group, begin by choosing your topic and the refrain (theme) of your ballad. Then tell the story. If you need help, raise your hand."

- Students will write ballads, receiving assistance from you as needed.

- After they have finished, they can share their ballads in small groups.

5. Closure

- "Now that you have written a ballad, what are the essential elements of a ballad?" Have a few students share their ballads with the entire class. Ask whether there are any questions and provide explanations as needed.

Poetry Example: **Ballad 1**

The Ballad of the Ducks

Mr. and Mrs. Mallard Duck
Were looking for a home.
They flew all over the clear blue sky
Until there was no place left to roam.
     Where are the ducklings going to live?
     Does anyone have any food to give?

Baton Rouge was the nearest town
A perfect place to spend the night.
They searched for food in the nearest pond,
But there was not a single fish in sight.
     Where are the ducklings going to live?
     Does anyone have any food to give?

They waddled through the busy city
Never finding a quiet place to rest
A policeman named Richard gave them peanuts.
He was, of course, the very best.
     Where are the ducklings going to live?
     Does anyone have any food to give?

Then one beautiful, sunny morning
Eight ducklings hatched in the park
Mr. and Mrs. Mallard were the proud parents.
But as for a home they were in the dark.
     Where are the ducklings going to live?
     Does anyone have any food to give?

Wandered throughout Baton Rouge
The ducks were looking for a home to land.
Then appearing before their eyes,
A tiny little island.
     Where are the ducklings going to live?
     Does anyone have any food to give?

Poetry Example: **Ballad 2**

Parker the Lonely Platypus

"My name is Parker and I need a friend,
Will someone stand by me to the end?"
Parker was a duck-billed platypus
Living in the forest by himself
One day Parker said, "I'm darn lonely,
It sure would be nice to have a friend."

"My name is Parker and I need a friend,
Will someone stand by me to the end?"
He walked on down to the riverside
And saw a duck swimming 'long the side.
"My name's Parker, would you like to play?"
But the duck said, "Sorry, I can't today."

"My name is Parker and I need a friend,
Will someone stand by me to the end?"
Then Parker walked on and met a beaver.
Workin' on her dam so he thought he'd meet her.
"Hey," said Parker, "can I give you a hand?"
"Thanks, but I'm O.K.," said the beaver.

"My name is Parker and I need a friend,
Will someone stand by me to the end?"
So Parker walked on feeling very sad
"I wish for a true friend to make me glad."
Suddenly Parker saw quite a nice sight—
'Twas another platypus in an awful plight.

"My name is Parker and I need a friend,
Will someone stand by me to the end?"
The platypus was looking so sad and blue.
Parker walked up and said, "How are you?"
She said, "I'm Anna and in need of a friend."
Parker said, "I'll stand by you until the end."

"My name is Parker and I need a friend,
Will someone stand by me to the end?"
So Parker and Anna stayed together
Talked all day and enjoyed the weather
And Parker isn't lonely anymore
Because he has Anna forevermore.

"My name is Parker and I need a friend,
Will someone stand by me to the end?"

Poetry Example: **Ballad 3**

The Ballad of Carswell Slate

At 7:00 A.M., from a long restful night
Carswell is awakened with a voice and a light,
"Time to get up." "Rise and shine"
But Carswell only whines, "I'm hungry, when do I dine?"

> From a distance "In a minute" is mumbled.
> Ah, "A minute's an hour," Carswell grumbled.

Finally at breakfast Carswell finds his place
While his four brothers and sisters feed their face.
Carswell gobbles his cereal and jumps on the floor,
Yells to his mother, "Can I have some more?"

> From a distance "In a minute" is mumbled.
> Ah, "A minute's an hour," Carswell grumbled.

After brushing his teeth and putting on his clothes
Carswell lies down on the couch for the cartoon shows.
A few hours pass while he lies on his back
He screams out loud, "When can I have a snack?"

> From a distance "In a minute" is mumbled.
> Ah, "A minute's an hour," Carswell grumbled.

After his snack, Carswell retreated to his room
Where he played with a gun that made a loud boom!
His eyes became heavy and he grew quite sleepy
Carswell then demands, "Mom, can you find my blankie?"

> From a distance "In a minute" is mumbled.
> Ah, "A minute's an hour," Carswell grumbled.

Dinner was wild with all the kids around
Carswell was sent to his room for being a clown
While in his room he spied a book with a monkey in a tree,
Carswell demands to mom, "I want a story read to me!"

> From a distance "In a minute" is mumbled.
> Ah, "A minute's an hour," Carswell grumbled.

The moon rises in the dark night sky
Carswell settles on his bed and is about to cry,
"Put on your pajamas before this book is read"
Carswell asks, "When is time for bed?"
From a distance "In a minute" is mumbled.
"Ah, a minute's an hour!" Carswell sighs.

Pre-Writing Worksheet: Ballads

1. Topic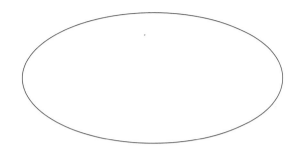

2. Refrain _____

_____

3. Stanzas

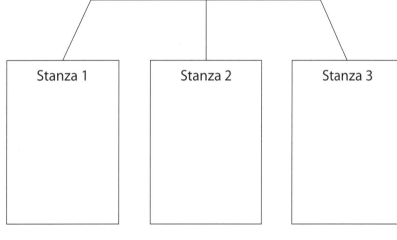

| Stanza 1 | Stanza 2 | Stanza 3 |

| Stanza 4 | Stanza 5 | Stanza 6 |

PART TWO

INTRODUCTION TO CHARACTERIZATION

In the previous lesson, students studied and wrote ballads. In writing ballads, students write a story, probably focusing on a character or set of characters. Writing ballads serves as an effective bridge to future lessons, because in the weeks ahead students will be writing narratives such as fables, fairy tales, spooky tales, and autobiographical sketches. Since students already like hearing and telling oral stories, they will probably enjoy these lessons.

In order to transition from poetry to narratives, however, and to develop concrete storytelling skills, in the next three lessons students will work on strategies that instruct them in developing characterization in narrative writing: writing *dialogue*, writing a *character sketch*, and writing a *biographical sketch*.

Dialogue instructs students that word choice reveals character, and it gives them practice adding concrete details to their writing. Writing a *character sketch* teaches students that observation is important to good writing, and helps students practice writing detailed examples for support. The biographical sketch draws on the same skills, but also asks students to incorporate outside resource material into a character sketch. These lessons are fun for student writers because they draw on students' experiences and interests, and they lend themselves to experimentation and exploration.

Characterization is essential to narrative writing because the relationship between characters, as well as the characters' own personalities, often determine the action of a story. Further, the process of writing dialogue or a character sketch teaches students to be observant about details when reading. This is active practice for close reading skills. Because they select settings, words, and appearance that reflect their characters' qualities, students gain a working understanding of figurative language.

In addition, people respond to other people. This is as true when readers read narratives as in real life. Learning to develop good characters enables students to write in a way that is appealing to readers, so they learn about audience issues. As a side benefit, in developing their own characters for narratives, students gain insight into human behavior.

Because people are interested in other people, students will have a natural interest in characterization. You, as the teacher, should draw on this innate curiosity about others to stimulate students' interest in the lessons. Remind students that they are already experienced in characterization. For example, you can refer to students' current favorite television series. Ask students about the setting of the series and what that suggests. Ask them about their favorite characters. How do they dress? Do they speak clichéd phrases ("that's hot") or have facial expressions that they use frequently? Ask students what such choices reveal about these characters.

From that point, you can ask students to examine either themselves or local figures—real people—and demonstrate that most people can be characterized if they are observed carefully. Finally, you can introduce this section by brainstorming with students an imaginary character, pointing out that a character living on the beach might say "dude" frequently, wear flip flops, and be laid back. Alternately, for contrast, the character and setting might be in opposition. (The character living on the beach might wear a tuxedo.) In either case, the objective is for students to understand that good characterization is a key ingredient to a good narrative.

Students are already familiar with characterization, even if unconsciously. Demonstrating that characterization is a part of students' daily lives will enable them to connect with this aspect of storytelling. These lessons build on students' ability to observe and write in detail.

DIALOGUES

A dialogue is the written record of the exact words spoken between two or more people. Dialogue adds personal style to a written text by allowing the reader to hear the person actually speaking. To do this effectively, the writer needs to use verbs and adjectives that vividly express the character's tone and emotion.

Dialogue is one of the few writing skills that teachers sometimes omit from their lessons. Dialogue should be introduced to students separately from an assignment that includes writing a paper or even a paragraph. Using the guidelines that follow, you can guide your students through the basic components of mastering dialogue and help them bring life to their writing.

Essential Elements

A dialogue

- Records the words spoken between two or more characters
- Begins a new paragraph each time a person speaks
- Uses verbs and adjectives to express tone and emotion
- Includes quotation marks around spoken words and ending punctuation inside quotation marks

Standards Dialogue Support

Writing dialogue supports many of the NCTE/IRA standards as described in the Introduction to Expressive Writing. In particular, students will produce conversations that develop the characters by demonstrating their actions and emotions.

Lesson Plan Example: Dialogue

Activity Objectives

In this lesson, students will

- Learn to recognize the essential elements of dialogue
- Develop effective and appropriate substitutes for the word "said"
- Write descriptive copy that supports and embellishes quoted material
- Demonstrate the ability to write descriptive dialogue

Activity Summary

The students will first learn the purpose and characteristics of dialogue. Students will then discover the importance of making a dialogue "come alive" by not overusing the word "said" and by describing the activities accompanying the dialogue. Students will then develop a dialogue as a group. Finally, students (working individually or in pairs) will write their own dialogues and share them with the group.

Materials
- Examples of dialogue (see the end of this lesson)
- A surface on which to write that can be easily seen by the entire class, such as a whiteboard

Description of Activities
1. Statement of Objectives
   - "Today we will work together on creating dialogue. Dialogue is a different style of writing from what you've learned in the poetry lesson. You will learn what the rules are for writing dialogue and how to write dialogue that paints a picture."

2. Class Discussion
   - Write the essential elements of dialogue on the board for the students to see:

     Records the words spoken between two or more characters

     Uses vivid verbs and adjectives to express tone and emotion

     Includes a new paragraph each time a person talks

     Includes quotation marks around spoken words

     Includes ending punctuation inside quotation marks

     Uses vivid verbs that capture emotion such as *chuckled, fretted,* or *shouted*

   - Read the list to the group, and make sure that the students understand each of the essential elements of dialogue.

- Explain to the students that the goal in writing dialogue is to have it sound natural—the way it would sound in real life. Also, they should provide descriptive words in the dialogues they write that allow the reader to "see" the scene. These descriptive words depict how the characters act while they're speaking.

- Students may be accustomed to writing formally. Point out to your students that the use of very formal writing can make dialogue sound boring and unnatural. In real life, you would not say: "I could never accomplish something that difficult; I am extremely awkward." Instead, you would say, "I could never do something that hard. I'm just too clumsy."

- When writing dialogue, it's natural for students to use the word "said" with great frequency. Point out to your students that dialogue can be boring and monotonous if the word "said" is overused. "Said" also doesn't convey any particular emotion or description. Suggest that your students try to use verbs that provide more information about *how* the speaker is saying the words.

- Write on the whiteboard (or display on a transparency) the following sentence of dialogue:

  "I could never do something that hard; I'm just too clumsy," said Billy.

- Now ask your students to notice the differences in the way they would interpret or "hear" the sentence if you simply change the verb, as follows:

  "I could never do something that hard; I'm just too clumsy," sighed Billy.

  "I could never do something that hard; I'm just too clumsy," cried Billy.

  "I could never do something that hard, I'm just too clumsy," laughed Billy.

- Ask the students to suggest some other alternatives. Write their suggestions on the board. (If they run out of ideas, there is a list of replacements for "said" at the end of this lesson. Suggest some of them to the class.) Ask the class what extra information the new words provide and when it might be appropriate to use them.

- "You can also have the character move in a way that expresses how he is feeling." Have students consider the following examples:

  Billy turned away, his shoulders slumped. "I could never do something that hard; I'm just too clumsy."

  Billy turned away and stamped his foot. "I could never do something that hard; I'm just too clumsy."

  Billy began to laugh. "I could never do something that hard; I'm just too clumsy."

- Point out to the class that none of these pieces of dialogue has any type of "said" word associated with it. The description is done in a separate sentence; the actual dialogue stands alone.

- Read Dialogue 1 (found at the end of the lesson) aloud to the students. (If possible, display the dialogue so the students can follow along as you read it.) Then read Dialogue 2 (also at the end of the lesson). Have them decide which of the two sounds more natural and what elements make that dialogue more believable.

- If time permits, display a dialogue (one of the other dialogues at the end of the lesson) so the entire class can easily view it. Have students read the displayed dialogue to themselves and then ask them, "What are some important things to consider when writing dialogue?"

- Have students read the same dialogue from the board, but this time aloud. Ask them, "How can we make dialogue sound more natural?"

3. Group Activity

- Ask the students to select a situation that involves dialogue. Have the group write a dialogue that fits that situation, with each student providing one sentence. (Where appropriate, encourage the students to provide a second, supporting sentence that describes the circumstances involving that particular line of dialogue.)

- Write the dialogue on the board as it is developed. When the dialogue is complete, read it aloud to the group.

4. Individual Activity

- Assign students to write their own dialogues at their desks. Students may work in pairs if they prefer. Tell them to raise their hands if they have any questions.

5. Closure

- Ask the students, "Now that you have written some dialogue yourselves, what do you think are the essential elements of dialogue?" If time permits, ask students to share the dialogues they wrote with the class.

Words to Replace "Said"

The word *said* can certainly be overused, but unwieldy and inappropriate replacements for *said* are not good writing. The following list gives some descriptive words that can be used—in the appropriate circumstance—instead of the word *said*. Think about what each of the replacement words means and why it is or is not appropriate for your situation.

admitted

announced

argued

bragged

cautioned

confessed

declared

expressed

hollered

insisted

insulted

interrupted

joked

laughed

ordered

pried

promised

snickered

spewed

stammered

stated

stuttered

suggested

whispered

Characterization Example: **Dialogue 1**

"Austin, you are very good at riding your bike with no hands," said Billy.

"Thank you, Billy. I have been trying for a long time to be able to ride my bike with no hands just so I can eat candy while I'm riding," Austin replied. "It is cool to be able to do that."

"How did you learn to do that? I could never do something that difficult. I am too clumsy," said Billy.

"My father says if you want something very much you have to be willing to take the steps necessary to attain your dreams. It took me a couple scrapes and lost teeth to learn this, but I'm sure you can too. I'll show you how I learned if you want," Austin offered.

"I'm not sure, Austin. I don't know if my mother would like me coming home all beat up. But she doesn't need to know. Let's give it a whirl!" Billy cried.

"All right, that's the spirit, Billy. Now I want you to sit on the seat and put your hands behind your back. I'll tie them together so you can't try to grab the bars. I'll push you down this hill. It's the biggest hill in town, but you're not scared, are you?" asked Austin.

"I'm not scared, Austin," Billy responded.

"Hang on tight!" screamed Austin.

Characterization Example: **Dialogue 2**

"Austin, you're awesome at riding your bike with no hands," said Billy.

"Thanks, Billy. I've been trying for a long time just so I can eat candy while I'm riding," Austin replied. "It's cool, isn't it?"

"I could never do something that hard; I'm too clumsy," sighed Billy. "How did you learn?

"My daddy says if you want something really bad you have to be willing to take the steps necessary to get it. I scraped my knees and lost two teeth, but I learned." Austin rolled up his jeans to reveal a bruised knee. "You can do it, too. I'll show you how."

"I don't know, Austin. My mom wouldn't like me coming home all beat up. But hey, she doesn't need to know. Let's give it a whirl!"

"All right, that's the spirit. Come over here and sit on the seat."

Billy walked over to the bike and climbed onto the seat.

"Now put your hands behind your back," Austin continued. "I'll tie them together so you can't grab the bars.

Billy put his arms slowly behind his back and looked down the hill. "Are you going to push me down that hill?" he asked.

"Sure. It's the biggest hill in town, but you're not scared, are you?" asked Austin.

"No, I'm not scared," Billy replied weakly. "Ready, set, go. Let 'er rip."

"Hang on tight!" screamed Austin.

Characterization Example: **Dialogue 3**

"Man, it's hot out here!" I told my friend, Colton, as we sat on the playground in the hot sun. "I'm ready to go inside."

"Me, too," replied Colton. "If I don't get something to drink, I think I'm just going to die! Maybe Mrs. Blackburn will let us go inside."

"Mrs. Blackburn," I asked, "may Colton and I go inside to cool off and get some water? Please, please, please! We're really hot!"

"No," she declared, "if I let you two go in, I have to let everyone else go in as well. It would not be fair to the other students. Besides, we're going inside in about five minutes. I think you can wait."

"But, Mrs. Blackburn," I complained, "I'm really, really hot, and I don't think that I can make it that long."

"No, KB!" she exclaimed. "Just go sit in the shade for five more minutes. I don't want to hear any more complaining. I'm hot, too."

"Mrs. Blackburn is the meanest teacher ever!" I told Colton.

"Yeah," Colton whispered, "I don't know why she won't let us go in alone. It's not like we're going to get in trouble or anything."

"I know. We never ever get into any trouble. She should let us do whatever we want because we're the best kids in the whole class!" I bragged.

Characterization Example: **Dialogue 4**

"Hi, how are you today? Are you looking for something specific?" the saleslady inquired.

"Yes, I am looking for a gift for my daughter for her birthday. I thought I would buy her an outfit. She's crazy about clothes."

"Dress or casual?" the clerk quizzed.

"Casual, maybe pants and a sweater."

"How old is your daughter?"

"Mel is sixteen."

"Mel. Is that short for Melinda?"

"Yes, it is."

"Do you like this pair of pants and this cardigan sweater? They're in style this year. What size is she?"

"Size five. I like the outfit, but I think she would prefer that red sweater with the black pants."

"That does go well together," she agreed. "I would be happy to wrap this for you if you like. Your total bill is $73.95. I hope your daughter likes her gift. Thank you for shopping with us."

CHARACTER SKETCHES

A character sketch allows students to analyze the main characters in their story entry. When you provide guidelines for character development, the student begins to think of the character as a real person and will begin adding personal qualities, experiences, and viewpoints to his or her writing, thereby delving deeper into their character development.

Using literary works and creating character analysis together with your students is an excellent introduction to characterization. The guidelines that follow also provide examples to use with your students.

Essential Elements

A character sketch

- Describes the qualities, experiences, or viewpoints of a real or fictional character
- May include descriptions of:

    Early life

    Growing up

    Important relationships

    Important events

    Personal beliefs

    Major accomplishments

    Contributions to society

- Literature-based sketches include a character's physical description, contributions to the story, importance to the story, and purpose

Standards Character Sketches Support

Character sketches support numerous NCTE/IRA standards, as described in the Introduction to Expressive Writing.

By writing a character sketch, students learn how to make written characters seem real to readers. In doing so, they increase their descriptive vocabulary, their ability to observe and analyze, and their understanding of the use of detail in writing.

Lesson Plan Example: Character Sketches

Activity Objectives

In this lesson, students will

- Demonstrate the importance of developing non-physical descriptions
- Write their own character sketches, based on people they know

Activity Summary

Students will see the purpose of a character sketch and will learn about and understand its essential elements. They will then read and analyze two character sketches. The students will develop a character sketch together, and then individual students (possibly working in small groups) will write their own character sketches.

Materials

- Examples of a character sketch (see the end of the lesson for two examples)
- A display surface to write on, such as a whiteboard, that all of the students can easily see
- A means of displaying a character sketch so that the entire group can read it (such as an overhead projector and screen, with the sketch written on transparencies or printed on handouts so that each member of the class reads an individual copy)

Description of Activities

1. Statement of Objective
   - "Today we will work together on character sketches. By the end of this lesson you will know how to construct your own character sketch."

2. Class Discussion
   - "Today we are going to learn how to write a character sketch." Point out the essential elements of a character sketch. A character sketch:

     Describes the qualities, experiences, or viewpoints of a real or fictional character

     May include descriptions of early life, growing up, important relationships, important events, personal beliefs, and/or major accomplishments and contributions to society

- Include a character's physical description, contributions to the story, importance to the story, and purpose, if they are literature-based sketches

- "A character sketch tells you about someone by describing him or her and his or her activities. The description often is not a physical portrayal—hair color or height—but rather a picture of what the person thinks and feels."

- Have the group read Character Sketch 1 (found at the end of the lesson). "After reading this character sketch, what can you tell me about Richard? What specific words or phrases led you to that conclusion?" Write the students' descriptions on the board.

- Now have the students read Character Sketch 2 (found at the end of the lesson). "After reading this character sketch, what can you tell me about Matt? Which words or phrases led you to that conclusion?" Make sure that all of the students realized that Matt is a dog. "What were the clues in the character sketch that indicated that Matt is not a human? At what point in the character sketch did you discover that Matt is a dog?"

3. Group Activity

   - "Now let's write a character sketch as a group." Have the students suggest a subject (not a fellow student) with whom all of them are familiar. (Possible subjects include a class pet, a school official, or a crossing guard.)

   - "What are some ways of describing this character?" List the descriptions on the board.

   - "Now let's combine these descriptions into a character sketch." Develop the character sketch on the board. If time does not permit writing the entire sketch, develop just the opening paragraph.

4. Independent Activity

   - "Now, I want you to write your own character sketches, writing about someone you know." Students may work individually or in small groups. Tell them to raise their hands if they have a question or problem.

5. Closure

   - When they are finished with their individual character sketches, ask students to share their character sketches with the group. Afterward, review the essential elements of a character sketch. "What are the important characteristics of a character sketch?"

Characterization Example: **Character Sketch 1**

Hard-working and unselfish are two words that fit Richard's personality. He sets his goals high, and settles for nothing less than achievement of those goals. As a child, he was brought up to respect other people and give of himself as much as possible.

He became very active in the Boy Scouts at a young age and served many leadership roles within his troop. At age 18, he became an Eagle Scout. His leadership in the Boy Scouts demonstrates how he gives his time to help others and his commitment to those organizations with which he becomes involved. He is dedicated and hardworking.

Richard believes that a person can do anything that he puts his mind to. When he was 15, his dad bought him a 1965 Ford Mustang coupe. The catch was that it didn't run at all. Richard dedicated every single weekend to working on the car and getting it to run. Just after his sixteenth birthday, he got the Mustang running and was able to drive it.

A month before he went away to college, he decided to restore the car by rebuilding the engine, painting the exterior, and making it look more presentable. Three years later, Richard is still working diligently on this project. His goal is to have it finished by college graduation. Given how important his goals are to him, without a doubt, he will be done by then.

Richard has formed an open and honest relationship with his parents and peers. His parents trust him to do the right thing and count on him to help them out. Many kids often receive an allowance for helping their parents out around the house, but in Richard's household, helping out was simply expected of him, and it was not something he did for extra money. At age 21, he still helps his parents around the house when he is home. He does not expect anything in return.

Richard's best feature, however, is his ability to make others laugh and enjoy life. No matter how hard things get, he sees the brighter side and can make most people laugh just by being silly. His parents enjoy the times when he is home because he makes them laugh. Even when he gets into mischief, it is hard for his parents to remain annoyed with Richard. He just looks up with his bright blue eyes, grins a funny grin, makes a quick retort, and they are over their irritation.

This is Richard's best trait and, potentially, his weakness—because he trusts that life will always go his way.

Characterization Example: **Character Sketch 2**

Two words that best describe Matt are loyal and guarded. He has been this way since he was young. Matt's parents abandoned him at the age of two, and he was placed in foster care. The only foster home available was with people who paid him no attention, and while Matt had food and shelter, he did not receive hugs and love and praise. After spending several years in this environment, Matt became very shy, but at the age of five he was fortunate to be chosen by his adoptive parents. Still, Matt was affected by his early history.

Matt considers the people he lives with as his family, and he tries his best to make his family happy, but he is always cautious when anyone new comes to the house until he is sure they are okay. Matt has a few odd habits. For example, he will stare fixedly at a piece of food, hoping his family will give it to him. He is also beside himself with joy whenever one of his family members returns to the house after a day at school or work. Another odd thing about Matt is that he loves cars. Whenever his mom goes someplace, Matt is the first one at the car door and will jump in quickly. Matt likes to eat, and he gets really excited when his mother puts ribs up in the crock-pot and he smells them cooking all day.

Mostly, however, Matt likes chasing cats. He hates cats because his foster parents owned a big orange tabby cat. This tabby cat had taken an instant dislike to Matt, hissing and spitting whenever he walked into a room. One day, the evil cat even got into Matt's food. His foster mom helped him, but not before the cat left a permanent scar on his hand. Now Matt thinks all cats are evil, so he chases them away. Although Matt works hard to please his family, his family isn't always pleased that he chases cats, and he sometimes gets into trouble for this. Matt only chases cats; he doesn't catch or hurt them.

Although five years later Matt is often shy and can't always express himself well, his best feature is probably his ability to sympathize with how his closest friends are feeling. He knows when they don't really have a lot to say, but he also knows instinctively when they have a lot to say, but just need to be encouraged to say it. He will just come up to his family members, rest his head on their legs, and wait patiently for them to say their piece. He is a good and loyal friend, and his life is now filled with hugs and love and praise.

BIOGRAPHICAL SKETCHES

A biographical sketch is a brief chronological summary of a person's life that is written in third person. The sketch includes major milestones of the person's life but goes beyond simply reporting facts to present the human side of the character.

Learning to use and design biographical sketches is a skill that students will draw on throughout their educational journey. Empowering students with the following essential elements will guide them to success from the start.

Essential Elements

A biographical sketch

- Is a concise chronological summary of a person's life written in the third person
- Tells about an individual's background, including his or her birth, death, family, friends, and interests
- Describes a person's accomplishments, education, work, and contributions to society
- Has interesting anecdotes (bits of information) that reflect the person's character
- Is written in a general paragraph format
- Contains the following pertinent information:

  Personal information

  Accomplishments

  Anecdotes

Standards Biographical Sketches Support

Character sketches support many NCTE/IRA standards, as described in the Introduction to Expressive Writing.

By writing a biographical sketch, students learn how to contrast the purposes and styles of a biographical sketch and a character sketch.

Lesson Plan Example: Biographical Sketches

Activity Objectives

In this lesson, students will

- Learn to recognize the essential elements of a biographical sketch
- Learn the difference between a biographical outline and a biographical sketch
- Write biographical sketches, both as a group activity and individually

Activity Summary

The students will first learn the essential elements of a biographical sketch. They will then compare a factual biographical outline with a biographical sketch and note the differences between the two. Given two biographical sketches, students will distill the factual information and create biographical outlines from them. Finally, students will write two biographical sketches, one as a group exercise and one individually.

Materials

- Examples of biographical sketches (see the end of this lesson)
- Biographical outlines of various famous people for students to work with in writing their own sketches (Encyclopedias and the Internet are good sources of factual material.)

Description of Activities

1. Statement of Objectives

   - "Today in class we are going to learn how to write a biographical sketch. You will see that a biographical sketch is similar in many respects to the character sketch that we explored previously."

2. Class Discussion

   - Explain to the students the essential elements of a biographical sketch. A biographical sketch:

     Is a concise chronological summary of a person's life written in the third person

     Tells about an individual's background, including his or her birth, death, family, friends, and interests

     Describes a person's accomplishments, education, work, and contributions to society

     Has interesting anecdotes (bits of info) that reflect the person's character, such as personal information, accomplishments, anecdotes

- Read the biographical outline of Abraham Lincoln (found at the end of this lesson) to your students. Then read the biographical sketch of Abraham Lincoln (also found at the end of this lesson.) "Which of these—the factual outline or the biographical sketch—told you more about Abraham Lincoln? Which of them was more enjoyable to listen to?"

- Now, working in reverse, have the students read the biographical sketch of George Washington and/or Dr. Martin Luther King Jr., and then have them write a short factual outline, based on the biographical sketch they just read.

- "Do you see the difference between a factual outline and a biographical sketch? Which conveys more information in a limited space? Which is more enjoyable to read?"

3. Group Activity

- Provide the students with biographical outlines of various famous people about whom they already know some details. Ask the students which of the people they would like to write a biographical sketch about. "How should our biographical sketch begin?" Write the first sentence or two of the biographical sketch on the board. If time permits, develop the remainder of the biographical sketch as a group.

4. Individual Activity

- "Now that you know how to write a biographical sketch, choose your own subject for a biographical sketch." Distribute the other biographical outlines to the students so that they can choose their favorites.

- Let the students know that you are there to help them if they need assistance. "If you have any questions or problems, raise your hand."

5. Closure

- Ask a few students to share their biographical sketches with the class. Ask if there are any questions. Review the essential elements of a biographical sketch.

Characterization Example: **Biographical Outline of Abraham Lincoln**

Personal Information
Birth: February 12, 1809

Death: April 9, 1865

A wife and four sons/two sons survived him

Personal Accomplishments
Taught himself law

Accepted to the state bar on March 1, 1837

Elected President of the United States in 1860 and again in 1865

Wrote and implemented the Emancipation Proclamation, freeing the slaves and making it illegal to own slaves in the states that had seceded

Anecdotal
It has been said that President Lincoln did more for this country than anyone else ever has.

Characterization Example: **Biographical Sketch 1**

Abraham Lincoln

Abraham Lincoln was born in Kentucky on February 12, 1809, in a one-room log cabin. His father nicknamed him Abe. Abe grew into a tall, lanky young man, who had a heart of gold. He was as strong as a horse, and his father would hire him out to the neighbors for 25 cents a day.

Abe was unable to go to school full-time like most kids today; instead, he had to work at home to help his family. He wanted an education, so he would work all day and study by lamplight at night. When Abe was 9, his mother died; a year later his father married his stepmother Sarah Bush Johnson, who had three children of her own. Abe like her and referred to her as "my angel mother" because she was always good to him.

Abe continued to study hard. On March 1, 1837, he was admitted to the state bar as a practicing attorney, which quickly gained him a junior partner title in the law office of Todd Stuart. Like many lawyers, Abe became interested in and started practicing politics. He was a member of the Illinois legislature, served in the U.S. House of Representatives, and ran against Stephen Douglas for U.S. Senator. Although he lost this race, his eloquent speeches won him attention and respect. He was nominated by the Republican Party for President of the United States in 1860.

In 1860, Abe won the election for the sixteenth President of the United States by a landslide. During this period, the country was going through a difficult time. By the time he was inaugurated, seven southern states had broken away from the Union to form their own government, The Confederate States of America. Lincoln attempted to pacify the South during his inaugural speech, for he was deeply against secession. On April 12, 1861, with the firing of Confederate troops on Fort Sumter, the Civil War began.

Many lives were lost during the war, which lasted almost four years. In the middle of the war, Abe wrote the now-famous Emancipation Proclamation, which made it illegal to own or possess slaves in the seceded Southern states. He delivered The Gettysburg Address, declaring the war a test of the ideals of a democratic nation, in 1863. This date also marked the beginning to the end of the war; however, many Southerners were still up in arms over the freeing of the slaves, and the country remained deeply divided.

On April 14, 1865, taking a short break from the more than four years of wartime stress, the president and the first lady attended a play at the local theater. While Mr. and Mrs. Abraham Lincoln were watching the play, a man named John Wilkes Booth came into their box and shot the president. As Abe slumped over, Mrs. Lincoln screamed, and everybody rushed to the president's side. Booth sprang from the box, breaking his leg in the jump, and got away. The president's unconscious body was carried across the street, and a doctor was sent for, but it was too late. At 7:22 A.M. on April 15, 1865, the day after General Lee's surrender at Appomattox Court House, Abraham Lincoln was dead.

Abraham Lincoln left behind a world in disbelief, a grief-stricken wife who never got over his death, two sons, and a legacy that has followed him for over 140 years.

It has been said that President Lincoln did more for this country than anyone else ever has. Indeed, the day of his assassination remains one of the saddest days in American history, but his legacy lives on today with the Civil Rights Movement.

Characterization Example: **Biographical Sketch 2**

George Washington

George Washington was born on February 22, 1732, in Westmoreland County in Virginia. He grew up in a big family with two older half-brothers and three younger brothers. Washington's father died when George was 11 years old. After the death of his father, he went to live with his half-brother Lawrence at Mount Vernon; Lawrence became a surrogate father for him. George had very little schooling, but taught himself to be an expert woodsman, surveyor (a person who determines the boundaries and areas of tracts of land), and mapmaker. Washington grew to be over 6 feet tall—which was very rare in Colonial times.

Years later, Washington settled in Mount Vernon, where he met Martha Curtis, whom he later married. At the age of 20, George joined the Virginia Militia as a major. He was a great success in the military and was chosen to be the army's leader in an effort to free the American people from the power of Great Britain. America wanted its independence. Washington was a great commander and finally helped America win the Revolutionary War. After this, many people wanted Washington to become the first President of the United States. Washington wanted no part of it. He only wanted to live peacefully at Mount Vernon.

The delegates (representatives) of the thirteen states were meeting in Philadelphia to write a Constitution for the United States. The Constitution declared that a president would be elected by the people to lead the new nation. Ballots were sent out, and the American people elected George Washington as their first president. George Washington served two terms as president, proving to be a very wise, caring, and fair leader.

After serving as the first President of the United States, he retired and spent the last three years of his life at Mount Vernon, the place he loved most. On December 14, 1799, George Washington died of a throat infection, after making a tour of his estate on horseback in very cold weather. George Washington left behind a nation in grief and a mournful wife. Two years later his wife died of a severe fever and was buried next to her husband in a plot at Mount Vernon.

It has been said that George Washington is our greatest president. He is responsible for establishing America as a free democratic nation. As first President of the United States, Washington set the standards for all future presidencies. He made the power of a president stand for the good of the American people. He will always and forever be remembered as an extraordinary leader in American history.

Characterization Example: **Biographical Sketch 3**

Dr. Martin Luther King Jr.

Dr. Martin Luther King Jr. was born on January 15, 1929, in Atlanta, Georgia. He was born into a small family that was supported by his father, who was an ordained pastor. Dr. King graduated from Booker T. Washington High School at the age of 15 and was accepted to Morehouse College in 1944. He graduated from Morehouse in 1948 and entered Crozer Theological Seminary at the age of 19. Like his father, Dr. King became an ordained Baptist minister. After his ordination on February 25, 1948, he entered Boston University for graduate studies.

In 1953, Dr. King found the love of his life and decided that he couldn't let Coretta Scott get away. So in the spring of 1953 he married Coretta in Montgomery, Alabama. Dr. King lived a quiet life with his new bride as he continued his schooling and received a Doctorate of Philosophy in Systematic Theology from Boston University on June 5, 1955.

On December 1, 1955, Dr. King joined a boycott that would become the driving force for the rest of his short life, and which would ultimately lead to his untimely demise. The boycott started because a woman on her way home from work did not want to give up her seat on a public bus. This courageous woman's name was Rosa Parks.

Dr. King continued the struggle for equal rights for blacks in America. His ideas and speeches were revolutionary for their time, and many people were motivated into action for a worthy cause by his talks. He believed in what he was doing, and everyone who followed him felt the same. Then one tragic evening on April 4, 1968, Dr. King was shot and killed while on his balcony at the Lorraine Motel in Memphis, Tennessee.

Although Dr. King has been dead for many years now, his beliefs still stand strong and his speeches still inspire many. He was an example of how to lead a movement and successfully change the course of history without shedding innocent blood or causing senseless violence in the process of progress.

PART THREE

INTRODUCTION TO NARRATIVE WRITING

Everyone loves a good story. People tell stories to entertain, to shed light on current problems, to provide insight into experiences, or to gain a better understanding of one another. People use narratives in formal and informal settings in order to connect with others and bridge the gap of experience. A good story can turn a stranger into a friend.

This section introduces students to narrative writing. Narrative writing recounts a personal or fictional experience or tells a story based on a real or imagined event. In well-written narration, a writer uses a combination of insight, creativity, drama, suspense, humor, and fantasy to create a central theme or impression. Narratives are generally told in chronological order, and stories usually include a distinct beginning, middle, and end. The following elements are found in narration: *characters, setting, plot* (conflict and resolution), and *theme.*

Narrative writing re-creates, manipulates, and interprets reality. Narrative writers must closely observe, explore, and reflect on a wide range of experiences. Narrative writing encourages creativity and speculation, and it offers writers an opportunity to understand their own emotions and actions, as well as those of others. This kind of writing encourages writers to narrate, reminisce, and imagine.

When students learn to write narratives, they learn to organize material in a chronological fashion; they learn to write a clear beginning, middle, and end of a story; and they learn to recognize and use the fictional elements such as character, setting, plot, and theme that make stories interesting to an audience. Narrative writing helps students develop good skills for organizing writing and good reading skills, and it gives them practice writing for an audience.

Students like stories, and many are already good storytellers; they just aren't used to writing stories. The lessons in this selection draw on the types of stories young readers are already familiar with and like: tall tales, short stories, fables, fairy tales, and spooky stories. While most will be excited by the chance to create their own tales, a few may be hesitant about writing their own stories.

Encourage students to share and brainstorm about funny moments, moments when they were scared (but that turned out okay), and times when they saw or heard something that seemed magical. This will help them relax and recognize that they have enough experience to write a narrative. Remind students that a narrative will "show, not tell," and that they can start writing their stories by pre-writing a character sketch or dialogue. This will build on earlier lessons and give students a place to start writing.

Narrative writing emphasizes the use of *elements of fiction* such as *plot, character, setting, dialogue, point of view, tone of voice,* and *figurative language.* Students have already worked on character and dialogue in the previous lessons. In addition, remind students that, when writing haiku, they used descriptive words to make a strong impact and that descriptions were also necessary for character sketches. Remind students that they have already written in more restrictive forms, such as poems. Now, they are going to have more freedom, but they must still write a beginning, middle, and end to their stories.

To demonstrate audience awareness and the need for plot, start narrating a story that has no introduction. Ask students how they felt. Then switch. Read a story that is exciting, but leave off the conclusion. Ask students how they felt when they were left without a conclusion. Then read the conclusion.

Ask students about the use of words in poems that stood for more than one thing. Discuss the use of figurative language in stories. Use one of the tall tale examples, such as "Big-Eyed Steve," to demonstrate that figurative language does not have to be serious to be effective.

Students will probably enjoy writing their own narratives; they have learned storytelling since childhood. Storytelling, or narrative writing, is an effective way to strengthen their writing skills.

TALL TALES

A tall tale is one of the most enjoyable forms of narrative writing for middle grade students. It is a short story that focuses on a larger-than-life character with unusual skills or abilities. Students can use their creativity to apply extreme exaggerations in their writings (hyperboles) that make the experience enjoyable.

Essential Elements

A tall tale

- Is a short story that exaggerates something that is normal
- Features larger-than-life characters with unusual skills and abilities
- Uses similes (using the words "like" or "as") in the description
- Revolves conflict resolution around the character's skills or unusual abilities
- Uses extreme exaggerations (hyperbole)
- Is usually humorous
- Is written in matter-of-fact, deadpan style that adds to the humor (being funny without trying)

Standards Tall Tales Support

Tall tales support many of the NCTE/IRA standards described in the Introduction to Expressive Writing.

When writing tall tales, students will learn to use humor and exaggeration for effect, and they will learn to decide what to exaggerate.

Lesson Plan Example: Tall Tales

Activity Objectives

In this lesson, students will

- Compose a variety of tall tales
- Produce work that follows the conventions of tall tales

Activity Summary

The students will hear a tall tale and then consider the essential elements that comprise tall tales. Then the students will see how pre-writing makes the actual writing of a tall tale easier. The class will pre-write a tall tale as a group, and possibly write the actual tall tale (time permitting). Finally, individual students will write their own tall tales, beginning by pre-writing and proceeding to the finished narrative.

Materials
- Ideas for tall tale characters (a suggested list is at the end of this lesson)
- Example of a pre-written tall tale (see the end of the lesson)
- Transparency of the pre-writing form
- Pre-writing forms for students (see end of the lesson)
- Sample tall tales (see the end of the lesson)
- Printed copies of the "Cletus Caesar Conway, the Wonder Cowboy" tall tale as class handouts
- Overhead projector

Description of Activities
1. Statement of Objectives
   - "Today, I am going to read a short tall tale for you. Then we will go through a guided pre-writing lesson, which will show you how you can design a tall tale. After that, you will write your own tall tales."
2. Class Discussion
   - Read the tall tale "Big-Eyed Steve" to the class. Ask: "What parts of this story really stood out to you?"
   - "Let's look at the essential elements of a tall tale." A tall tale:

     Is a short story that exaggerates something that is normal

     Features larger-than-life characters with unusual skills and abilities

     Is usually described with similes (like, as)

     Revolves conflict resolution around the character's skills or unusual abilities

Uses extreme exaggerations (hyperbole)

Is usually humorous

Is written in matter-of-fact, deadpan style that adds to the humor (being funny without trying)

- "Does the story I just read include all of these elements?"

- "A good way to begin to write a tall tale is to start with a 'pre-write.'" Show students the sample pre-write for a tall tale on the overhead projector. Have students examine the different parts of the pre-write. "Do you have an idea of what the tall tale might look like, based on this pre-write?"

- Now distribute the "Cletus Caesar Conway, the Wonder Cowboy" tall tale to the class. Pick different students to read just one paragraph each aloud to the other students. When the tall tale has been read, ask the students how this tall tale compared to their expectations from the pre-written sample.

3. Group Activity

- "Now we'll write our own tall tale. First, let's do a pre-write together." Place a transparency with the pre-write outline on the overhead project. (Also distribute the outline to the students as a worksheet.)

- With students sitting in pods of two or three, give each pod a different part of the pre-write to do as you work through it together.

- Ask the first pod to come up with a title for the tall tale. "When thinking of a title and theme, remember that the character must have unusual skill, abilities, and/or features. This will shape the rest of the story." If they have trouble selecting a theme, give them a list of ideas (see the list of tall tale character ideas at the end of the lesson). As they say their ideas aloud, write them down.

- The next pod will come up with the characters in the tall tale. Write these down, and so on. (It is almost like doing a chain story, but with a pre-write.)

- Have them write the group-developed details on their worksheets as you proceed. This will later serve as a reference when they do first drafts of their own stories.

- "Now that we have an outline, filling in the story will be easy." If time permits, have the students develop their tall tale, one sentence at a time. When the tall tale is finished, read the entire story to the class.

4. Individual Activity

- After completing the group pre-write, have students do pre-writes of their own. "You can now work on your own pre-writes. Fill in the important information about your tall tale. This will make writing your tall tale much easier." Distribute blank pre-write worksheets for them to use during this independent practice and the sample worksheet as an example.

- "When you are finished with your pre-writes, I want you to begin working on your tall tales." Since this is narrative writing, students will be familiar with the beginning, middle, and end. They should be able to fill in the paragraphs easily once they have outlines.

- Once students have finished writing their tall tales, have them read them aloud to the class.

5. Closure

- "You have successfully written a tall tale, your first example of narrative writing." Review the essential elements of a tall tale.

Tall Tale Character Ideas

Tall tales are frequently written around the adventures of a "bigger-than-life" individual. Here are some ideas for colorful characters that students may wish to use for their own tall tales.

It is important that students base their tall tales on fictional characters, like the ones listed here. There can be a temptation to use a real person, especially a classmate, in writing a tall tale. You should discourage students from using real people in their tall tales, as hurt feelings can easily result.

Jimmy the Giant	Cry Baby Bell
Sandy Sea Breeze	Jake the Snake
Larry Long Arms	Stevey Big Boots
Big-Eyed Steve	Dapper Joe
Barney Big Ears	Strong Arm Sam
Tall Tim Timber	Will the Weatherman
Big Hand Hank	Steven Stretchable
Tran S. Lucent (translucent)	Ralph Runny Nose
Big Mouth Mandy	Phillip Long Legs
Slim Stretching Stan	Mouthy Mae
Junnah with the Big Ears	Katrina, the Wannabe Ballerina
Matt "Monkey" Mason	Bigfoot Fred
Bailey Brook Bear	Rudy Rooster
Side Whistling Willy	Big Billy Steve Bicep
Hanna Harriet Hen	Long Hair Lucy
Wilma Big Wheels	Buck Tooth Billy
Silly Sarah Sills	Mr. Noah Nosey
Tiny Timmy Tucker	Gary Green Thumb

Name _____ Date _____

Pre-Writing Sample Worksheet: Tall Tales

Title, Theme: Cletus Caesar Conway, the Wonder Cowboy
_____

_____

Characters: Cletus Caesar Conway, Cows, Cletus's Mother, Townsfolk
_____

_____

Setting: Texas countryside
_____

_____

Unique Ability: 40-foot-tall human
_____

_____

Major accomplishment of the character: Saved the state of Texas; Gained respect
from townsfolk
_____

_____

Exaggerations and hyperbole; bigger than life: 40-foot-tall man and cows; nuclear
meltdown
_____

_____

Conflict: A nuclear meltdown that mutated cows, which almost destroyed the town
_____

_____

Resolution: Cletus saved the town from being destroyed by the 40-foot cows
_____

_____

Pre-Writing Worksheet: Tall Tales

Title, Theme: _____

_____

_____

Characters: _____

_____

_____

Setting: _____

_____

_____

Unique Ability: _____

_____

_____

Major accomplishment of the character: _____

_____

_____

Exaggerations and hyperbole; bigger than life: _____

_____

_____

Conflict: _____

_____

_____

Resolution: _____

_____

_____

Narrative Writing Example: **Tall Tale 1**

Cletus Caesar Conway, the Wonder Cowboy

A while back in the foothills of Texas lived Cletus Caesar Conway. He was a regular looking cowboy, that is, until he stood up. When Cletus stood tall, people just about broke their necks looking up to see him, because he stood 40 feet tall from foot to head. All of the townsfolk loved to tease Cletus. They would ask "How's the weather up there, Cletus," or "Does the altitude make your nose bleed?" No matter what the joke of the day was, Cletus was always at the top of their list. Poor Cletus, he would just hold his head low as he walked away.

At the age of 25, Cletus still lived with his parents on the outskirts of town, for two reasons. First, nobody else wanted him; second, throughout Cletus's growing years his parents had obliged him by extending the roof to 42 feet so that he could walk through the house without bumping his head. On Sundays when Cletus would go to church, he would have to sit outside and listen to the service, but that didn't deter him. He never missed a Sunday service, that is, unless it rained. It was hard for Cletus to get a job in town because he couldn't get into the buildings or the factories. The townsfolk were scared to hire him because they feared he would cause more damage than good.

Lo and behold, about this time a dreaded cow disease was sweeping through Texas. It was wiping out whole herds, and if the ranchers happened to eat the meat of sick cows, they too would die. One night the Texas Exchange, a nearby nuclear plant, had a meltdown and radiation was sweeping the countryside, enveloping everything in its path, including (of course) the cows.

The next morning the ranchers woke to a herd of 40-foot cows with the dreaded cow disease. The radiation leak had mutated the cows, and they were trampling and destroying everything in their path. Oh, no! What are the ranchers to do? They'll all be killed! Texas will be wiped off the map. All of a sudden, one of the ranchers spoke up and said, "Let's get Cletus. Maybe he can help us!"

As they drove up to Cletus's house, they were constantly dodging raging cows. When they reached Cletus's door, his mother answered and told them to go away, that they had been too mean to Cletus to expect him to help them now. However, Cletus overheard the conversation and offered to go and help them. Cletus's mother asked, "Son, why would you chance risking your life on people who have mistreated you all of your life?" Cletus took his mother by the arm ever so gently and led her to the kitchen table, reminding her that she had raised him to be a good person and that they needed his help.

Cletus took off in the direction where the cows were last seen. As he approached them, the bulls attacked him first. As they came charging, Cletus hit each bull one time square in the face, and each one was turned into hamburger, ribs, steaks, and roasts. Cletus continued until all of the cows were destroyed. By the time Cletus was done with the cows, there was enough meat to feed Texas for the next 200 years. The mutation had in fact killed the dreaded cow disease, and now the cows were safe to eat again.

The townsfolk praised and cheered Cletus for his heroic feats, promising never again to make fun of him and to restructure the town so that Cletus could visit or patronize any place in the whole state of Texas.

Narrative Writing Example: **Tall Tale 2**

Big-Eyed Steve

There once was a very famous and feared pirate by the name of Big-Eyed Steve. He had grown up on the sea and was known as the best lookout in the known world. This was due to his extremely keen eyesight that the good lord had given him. You see, Big-Eyed Steve had an eye that was about the size of a cantaloupe, and some say he could see better than a hawk and an owl combined.

Steve was offered a job as lookout on a Spanish galleon that was bound for India to do some commercial trading. Now to all you landlubbers who have never been aboard a Spanish galleon, let me tell you, it is a sight to be seen. The fine Spanish oak polished to a keen shine and the beautiful linen used to make the sails are sights that all should enjoy at least once in their lifetimes.

Now the captain of the Spanish galleon was Captain Arrg, and he was a very good captain, but he believed that talking was unnecessary, so all he said was "Arrrg." Captain Arrg had a full crew, and they were a very good crew. They all took a liking to Big-Eyed Steve quickly; that is, all except one. Jaguar had liked to climb the mast and be the lookout, but Big-Eyed Steve had better eyesight, so Jaguar had to swab the decks instead.

The Spanish galleon headed out on its long voyage to India, and everything was great for Steve. He got to sit in the outlook bucket and listen to the captain shout out orders. "ARRRRRGGG," shouted Captain Arrg, and all the crew manned the sails and caught a good wind. Now every chance that Jaguar got he would try and get the rest of the crew to hate Big-Eyed Steve because Jaguar wanted to have him swabbing the decks while Jaguar was in the lookout bucket. No matter how hard he tried though, the crew still liked Big-Eyed Steve. He could see land miles before it came into sight to the rest of the crew, and they loved Steve for this. So Jaguar devised a plan to hurt Big-Eyed Steve.

Jaguar knew that Steve's eye was so big that he needed to put drops in it a lot to keep the salt air from drying it out and so Jaguar decided to slip some honey into his eye drops. Then a bee would think that Steve's eye was a beehive and would fly right into it. So late one night when everyone was asleep, Jaguar did the horrible deed and then went to his bunk snickering, knowing that if Steve couldn't be lookout, he would be.

Sure enough, the next day Big-Eyed Steve was on lookout when he let out a horrible scream. A bee had flown into his eye. Steve was taken to the ship's doctor and his eye was patched up, but he wouldn't be able to do lookout duty for a while. So Captain Arrg gave out a terrible "AAAAARRRRRRRRRRGG," which told Jaguar to man the lookout bucket. The crew was very distressed, as this was a sign of bad luck ahead. The captain reassured his crew with a compassionate "Arrrg."

Well, the crew's fears were correct. By nightfall, a horrible storm began to brew up. All the crew was busy preparing the ship by lashing everything down tightly. Steve helped the best he could, but with the big patch over his eye he got in the way more than anything. Jaguar took every opportunity to make fun of Steve's predicament.

When the storm hit, all went below deck, except for Jaguar, who had to remain in the bucket to look for other ships or land. Well, as the storm continued to crash against the boat, a fog began to move in and Jaguar could see nothing at all. The boat continued to rock and sway, and suddenly Jaguar lost his footing and slipped and hit his knee against the bucket. He fell to the floor with a broken leg. Jaguar could no longer be the lookout. The rest of the crew was below deck and did not know of Jaguar's predicament. They continued to wait out the storm and fog.

Suddenly, the whole crew heard a foghorn, and they all went above deck. Somehow the boat had been blown back toward land and was dangerously close to rocks. The fog was so thick that the light from the nearby lighthouse could not be seen, so the owner was using a foghorn and Morse code to alert sailing vessels to steer clear. The crew shouted to ask Jaguar to tell them which direction the foghorn was coming from, but he couldn't stand up to find out. The captain began to shout orders, but the storm was so loud no one could hear. The crew just stood there in fear of the rocks, not knowing where they were.

Big-Eyed Steve immediately went up on deck to help out. He knew that if he tore off the patches he could see through the fog and tell the captain which way to steer to avoid the rocks. So without thinking about his own safety, Big-Eyed Steve tore off his patches and began to climb the mast to the lookout bucket. The salt air and rain began to sting his huge sore eye almost immediately, but Steve ignored the pain and reached the top. When he climbed into the bucket, he saw Jaguar in pain and tried to make him more comfortable. Steve strained his keen eyesight to see through the fog. After a few seconds, he was able to see the lighthouse and told the captain to steer to the right to avoid the jagged rocks in front of them.

The galleon was turned just in time to avoid disaster. Steve helped Jaguar down from the lookout bucket and into the doctor's room, where Jaguar's leg was set. The storm subsided and everybody cheered for Big-Eyed Steve, who had saved the ship with his enormous eye and keen eyesight.   The ship made it to India, where they traded some of the best things that they had ever seen and received twenty gold coins for every crewmember. Steve was promoted to first mate, and Jaguar and he became very close friends. From then on, they frequently shared the lookout bucket.

Narrative Writing Example: **Tall Tale 3**

Gnarly Jason: A Tall Tale of a Surfer

Jason is the best surfer in Hawaii; in fact, some people say he is the best surfer in the United States, and some even say he is the best in the world. Jason looks just like any other surfer, with blond hair and tanned skin. Jason is really strong; one time he even helped an old woman by picking up her car and freeing a kitten trapped underneath. Jason was always helping out, whenever he was not surfing. He surfed all the time. If there were gnarly waves, Jason was there. Everyone called him Gnarly Jason because he could ride all the gnarly waves—the big, strong ones, that is.

One day Brodie, Jason's best friend, told Jason that the president of the United States was coming to their town for vacation. Jason had never met President Max Adams before, but President Adams wanted to see Jason surf. Jason sure was nervous, but he told Brodie he would be surfing in an hour if President Adams wanted to watch. Sure enough, the president and Jason were out on the beach one hour later. The president brought his daughter, Roxie, along to watch. Roxie didn't care much for surfing, so she decided to go for a swim.

President Adams watched Jason ride one wave after another. Brodie said the waves were bigger than ever before that day. All of a sudden, out of nowhere, a raging rip current came thrashing through the water. Roxie was swept away. But she did not panic; she just zoomed away. "Look" shouted President Adams to Jason, "Roxie is gone! Please help, Jason!"

At the same time, a wave swelled up, the biggest wave Gnarly Jason had EVER seen. He paddled, stood up, and then he rode the wave; he rode that wave for miles and miles. After going for longer than Jason could keep up with, he saw Roxie. She had finally ridden the rip current out to the end and was treading water. Jason rode right up to Roxie and told her to hop onboard. Now here is the part that is unbelievable: That wave switched directions and Gnarly Jason rode that wave all the way back to the other side of the island to the president.

President Adams was so shocked that he passed out, seeing Roxie on the surfboard with Jason on one gnarly wave.

When President Adams came to, he saw Roxie and Jason looking down at him. Roxie was so happy that her father was all right, and the president could not have been happier to see his daughter safe and sound.

Brodie came running up to see what was going on. He was shouting about that gnarly wave Jason was riding. "That wave was 1,000 feet high!!" Brodie was yelling. Nobody could believe it, not even Jason! Could you?

Narrative Writing Example: **Tall Tale 4**

Rocky, the Salt Boy

Not too long ago, a boy was born with two extremely rare diseases. One caused him to grow to be extremely large, and the other gave him an incredible appetite for hot, spicy, and salty foods. In fact, he needed tremendous amounts of spicy, salty foods just to live. Instead of milk or baby food, he was fed large amounts of Tabasco sauce, habañero juice, and bags of salt. Initially, his parents were overwhelmed and worried about the new baby, but he was a very happy baby and smiled a lot, so they decided not to make a big deal about it and simply named him Rocky.

By the time Rocky was 16 years old, he was over 60 feet tall and needed several dozen 50-pound bags of salt per day and barrels of hot sauce from all over the world just to satisfy him. Nothing seemed too hot or spicy or salty to him. He craved salt and spices and needed them for his body to function.

Rocky was a kind and gentle boy, but his size and appetite intimidated some people and downright scared most. Everywhere he went, people ran away from him, not just because of his size but also because of his hot, spicy breath, which would melt asphalt roads and fry trees to a crisp if he burped too close to the ground. And worst of all, if Rocky had gas, he had to make sure there was nothing living behind him for about two miles or "Whew!!!" People and animals would pass out for hours, and plants would wilt and die. Poor Rocky would never hurt a fly, but he had a hard time making and keeping friends. Most people just ran away or locked themselves in their homes when they saw him coming, so he spent most of his time alone near the ocean, drinking thousands of gallons of nice salty ocean water when he was thirsty.

One warm summer day, a nasty dictator from an evil country decided to attack the United States. He sent a huge chemical bomb over on a ship and then had the ship blown up near the beach of a large Eastern city. When the large chemical cloud was seen approaching the city, everyone panicked and started running for their lives. What were they to do? There weren't enough gas masks for these millions of people, and most were sure to die when the cloud reached them. No one knew what to do.

No one except Rocky. Rocky grabbed a huge metal pipe and ran toward the beach. He figured that if all the salt and spice that he ate every day could not harm him, then maybe his body could also absorb this strange cloud also. Plus, he knew that salt was a natural filter for many foreign products, and he knew his body was so saturated with salt that it might just act like a big filter so the chemicals couldn't harm him.

When he got to the beach, he ran into the water, put the pipe in his mouth and started to suck in as much of the chemical cloud as he could. He filled his huge lungs and then dove into the water and exhaled it all away into a harmless mixture of gas and salt water. He came back up and did this several times until there wasn't one wisp of chemical cloud left in the air. When all the chemicals were out of the air, Rocky felt quite fine until he was walking back toward the beach and felt that he had to pass some gas, so he went back under the water and "whoosh," let it all go. The ocean turned into one big Jacuzzi for about five miles for the next two minutes. But no one cared because Rocky had saved them all.

After that, everyone loved Rocky and people would deliver truckloads of hot, spicy, salty foods to Rocky's home. They just brought their gas masks with them, and when Rocky gave them a friendly warning, they put them on until Rocky smiled and said, "All clear."

SHORT STORIES

A short story contains the same four components as other narrative works: characters, setting, plot, and theme. A short story begins with an introduction that quickly grabs the reader's attention, introduces the main characters, and presents the setting in a flowing manner. In addition, a short story has a unique conflict that intensifies and builds interest as the plot thickens. A short story has a climax when the plot reaches its peak and then flows into the conclusion of the story.

Essential Elements

A short story

- Has an introduction that grabs the reader's attention, establishes a setting, and introduces the main character
- Has an interesting conflict that heightens interest as the plot develops
- Has a conflict that falls into one of three categories: *character versus character, character versus self,* or *character versus nature*
- Includes a single event called the "climax," which is the peak of the interest level
- Ends with a conclusion that follows resolution of the conflict
- Has a resolution that often surprises the reader with a twist or cliffhanger

Standards Short Stories Support

Like other narrative writing, short stories support many of the NCTE/IRA standards, as described in the Introduction to Expressive Writing.

Students will understand the purpose and steps to creating a climax in a story. Students will identify and utilize the components of a story (such as the introduction, setting, characters, plot, and climax).

Lesson Plan Example: Short Stories

Activity Objectives

Students will compose first drafts using an appropriate writing process:

- Planning and drafting
- Rereading for meaning
- Revising to clarify and refine writing with guided discussion

In this lesson, students will

- Consider the essential elements of a short story
- Pre-write a short story
- Write their own short stories

Activity Summary

Students will begin by considering the essential elements of short stories. They will then compile lists of descriptive words and transitional words that they can use in writing their own short stories. They will discover how pre-writing eases the development of a story, and then they will outline and write their own short stories.

Materials

- Examples of short stories (see the end of this lesson)
- Transparency of "The Ducks' Home" pre-written outline
- Overhead projector

Description of Activities

1. Statement of Objectives
   - "Today you will consider one of the most popular forms of narrative writing—the short story. You will then see how to pre-write a short story. Finally, you will write your own short stories."
2. Class Discussion
   - "You have probably already read some short stories. Which short stories can you remember?" Ask the responders why they remember those particular stories.
   - "Now that we are preparing to write short stories, you need to know the important parts that go into a short story." A short story:

     Has an introduction that grabs the reader's attention, establishes a setting, and introduces the main character

Has an interesting conflict that heightens interest as the plot develops

Has a conflict that falls into one of three categories: character versus character, character versus self, or character versus nature

Includes a single event called the "climax," which is the peak of the interest level

Ends with a conclusion that follows resolution of the conflict

Has a resolution that often surprises the reader with a twist or cliffhanger

- "When you write your own short stories, remember that you are expected to use descriptive words and phrases to 'paint pictures' in the minds of your readers. You also need to use transition words to move the reader's attention along. And you need to have at least eight sentences in the short stories that you'll be writing for this class.

- "As with tall tales, it is helpful in writing your short story if you define the important parts of the story in a pre-write." Distribute blank copies of the pre-write forms to the students.

- "Let's see how a pre-write relates to the resulting short story." Put a transparency of "The Ducks' Home" pre-writing example on the over-head projector. Show the different parts of the pre-write to the class, including the name of the short story and the names of the characters, setting, conflict, and how the conflict will be solved. Explain why those parts of the story are important.

- "Now let's read 'The Ducks' Home' short story and compare it to the pre-write." Distribute copies of "The Ducks' Home" and read the story aloud to the class. Ask the class to identify effective descriptive and transitional words that were used in the short story.

3. Group Activity

- "Now let's write our own short stories. We will work on these over the next few classes. To begin, let's develop a list of descriptive words that you can use in your own short stories." Encourage the class to suggest descriptive words. Compile a list of the most descriptive words on the board.

- "Now let's develop a list of transitional words that you can use in your short stories." Encourage the class to suggest transitional words, and write the best suggestions on the board.

- Use the Imaginative Narrative Prompts at the end of the book to develop a list of possible story choices. Write the possible story themes on the board (or on a transparency) for the class to see. "Here are some possible story choices. Look them over and select a theme that you would like to use for your short story."

- "Now go through our earlier lists of descriptive words and transitional words and select those that you think will be most useful in writing the short story that you've selected. If you can think of any other descriptive or transitional words, you can add them to your list."

4. Individual Activity

- "Let's do the pre-write for your short story. Let's start with the characters and the story's setting." Distribute the pre-writing worksheet and the sample filled-out worksheet to serve as an example. Have the students write down the name(s) of the main character(s) in their short stories and the setting.

- "Now describe the main problem your main character will solve." Have the students write down what problem (conflict) the main character will face.

- "How will you solve that problem?" Have the students write down how they are going to solve the problem (conflict).

- "Now write the beginning of your short story." Have the students write the first sentences of their short stories.

- "Over the next few classes, you will continue to develop your short stories." Have the students keep all of their work in their "writing folders."

5. Closure

- When the students have finished writing their short stories, have them share them with their classmates by reading them aloud.

Name _____   Date _____

Pre-Writing Sample Worksheet: Short Stories

Story Title: <u>The Ducks' Home</u>

_____

_____

_____

Describe Setting: <u>a beautiful lake with bridges and grassy banks, set in the</u>

<u>middle of a tourist area</u>

_____

_____

Characters: <u>Quackers, Jack, Lucky, and Mally, who are all ducks; also the tourists</u>

<u>of the area</u>

_____

_____

Main Conflict: <u>People are polluting the lake and teasing the ducks</u>

_____

_____

_____

Obstacles to Overcome: <u>Quackers's sister getting hit by an aluminum can;</u>

<u>pollution of the lake</u>

_____

_____

How to Overcome Obstacles: <u>All ducks in the lake swarm and peck at anyone who</u>

<u>decides to pollute the lake or tease the animals</u>

_____

_____

_____

Name _____ Date _____

Pre-Writing Worksheet: Short Stories

Story Title: _____

_____

_____

_____

Describe Setting: _____

_____

_____

_____

Characters: _____

_____

_____

_____

Main Conflict: _____

_____

_____

_____

Obstacles to Overcome: _____

_____

_____

_____

How to Overcome Obstacles: _____

_____

_____

_____

Narrative Writing Example: **Short Story 1**

The Ducks' Home

"Quack quack! Coming through," called Quackers as he and his duck friends made their way across the busy lake. Quackers and his friends, Jack, Lucky, and Mally, lived near a big tourist area in South Carolina. All day they would swim around the lake while people walked around them. The four ducks loved swimming around this lake, especially on a nice, warm, sunny day. There were bridges for shelter but also wide-open spaces for swimming and playing. There were also nice, quiet, grassy areas where mother ducks could rest and lay eggs. The ducks got plenty of attention and food. It was the perfect place for a home . . . or so they thought.

But there was a big problem. The tourists who visited this area didn't know how to treat the ducks and other animals of the lake. They tried to spit on them from on top of the bridges. They chased down the ducks and bribed them with food, only to hurt them. The worst part, though, was that people threw trash and nasty liquids into the lake, as if Quackers and his friends and family didn't live there. Quackers and his friends were getting mad, but they weren't exactly sure what they could do.

One day, a little boy walking by thought it would be funny to throw an aluminum can at the ducks. He just happened to hit Quackers's little sister Mally. "Alert, alert!" Quackers called out to Jack and Lucky. "Alert, alert!" Jack and Lucky called out to all of their duck friends. All of a sudden, a swarm of ducks came charging at the boy and the people near him. They'd had enough. No more polluting and no more teasing! They pecked at the little boy just like he had picked on the ducks.

From this day on, any time the ducks caught someone polluting the lake or teasing the other animals, they would swarm the person. The humans finally understood what was going on and stopped polluting the lake and teasing the animals. They posted warning signs around the lake: "WARNING: These ducks seem peaceful, but they are dangerous when teased, or when objects are thrown into the lake." Once they began defending their home, the ducks on this lake lived a peaceful and clean life.

Narrative Writing Example: **Short Story 2**

Mahnoa and the Black Tips

On a small island in the southern Pacific Ocean, there was a small fishing community in which many of the people enjoyed surfing. A boy by the name of Mahnoa who lived there loved to surf. Mahnoa could only surf after he helped his fisherman father with the daily chores of untangling the net and setting the rigs to cast.

An elite group of surfers in this village was made up of the best from the entire chain of islands. They called themselves the "Black Tips." They were a very close group, and did not encourage new members. Only the best surfers on the islands were even considered. Mahnoa had wanted to be a part of this great group since he was a little boy. Now at 13, he was almost a man, and he was ready to claim his membership in the Black Tips.

Every day Mahnoa surfed harder than any other person. He pretended that he was in the tryouts and that each set was the best one of the day. He dropped into every wave with a determination not just to surf, but to ride the wave and learn all he could from each one. Mahnoa believed that each wave carried a lesson, either about surfing or about life. He wanted to learn every one and become the best Black Tip ever.

One day while practicing for the tryouts, Mahnoa began paddling for a wave when suddenly someone began yelling at him from way down the line. It was Kaluah, one of the best Black Tips out that day. Mahnoa tried his best to pull off the wave, but it began to bowl up and he was sent sprawling over the falls. Kaluah saw this all happening and tucked into the barrel and tried to beat past Mahnoa, but he failed and went out the back of the wave.

Other surfers heard the commotion and paddled toward Kaluah and Mahnoa to see what was going on. Mahnoa was trying to apologize and calm Kaluah down. Kaluah was very upset, since Mahnoa had almost caused him to be dragged across the reef. All the Black Tips heard the happenings and marked Mahnoa as someone who was far too rude and selfish to ever be considered as a Black Tip candidate.

Mahnoa was crushed. He had been working for so long to become a member. He looked up to so many of them, and now he had been shamed in front of everybody. He went back and told his father the horrible news. His father, a very wise and seasoned longboarder, reminded Mahnoa that all things work themselves out in the end and that worrying about them can change nothing but the hair color on your head. Mahnoa thought long and hard and decided that the next swell he would paddle out and surf his best and be extra-special careful to look down the line before going for the drop. He would not let this little bump deter him from his ultimate goal of becoming a Black Tip.

So Mahnoa helped his father out, patiently waiting for the next swell in which somehow he would be able to redeem himself. His wish came true early on a Thursday morning. The swell was from the southeast. Mahnoa paddled out at the same spot and saw all the same people. Today, they were blocking him out of the main break as best they could. He moved into the lineup and waited his turn. Kaluah was eying him warily from about ten positions down the line.

Suddenly a huge swell came through and Kaluah got the third wave of the set. It was a big wave, and it was bowling up quickly along the reef. He set up for the barrel and got way back into it, when suddenly the window closed and the whole barrel closed out. Kaluah was dragged along the reef for about ten feet. Mahnoa saw this before anyone else and immediately caught the next wave in and dove in right where Kaluah had fallen. Manoah grabbed Kaluah and brought him to the surface. Mahnoa continued to swim, keeping the unconscious Kaluah safe from the waves until the rest of the huge set passed through. Each time a wave passed by, Mahnoa took Kaluah's limp body and dived deep with it as the wave went by. The Black Tips who saw this were astounded at the courage and skill Mahnoa showed.

When the set finally passed, Mahnoa brought Kaluah's body to shore and revived him quickly. The Black Tips made a unanimous decision right there on the beach to make Mahnoa one of them.

Mahnoa felt so proud that finally he was part of the Black Tips.

FABLES

Fables come from the oral tradition of storytelling found in folklore around the world. Many cultures encapsulated their heritage through this type of storytelling. A fable is a short, whimsical tale with characters that are often personified (animals or objects that take on human characteristics). It is structured around an introduction, a problem or conflict, the resolution or attempt at resolution, and an outcome. Generally fables teach a lesson about life and end with a "moral to the story" that sums up the lesson.

Fables are an excellent way to teach imaginative narratives (which are tested in most states in grade 4 or 5). Students often have difficulty creating the problem or conflict in the narratives. Using fables, especially with the pre-write planning charts, ensures they include all of the required components. In addition, students enjoy the playful elements of fables.

Essential Elements

A fable
- Is a brief, fanciful tale
- Has characters, often including animals that act or talk like people (personification)
- Has an introduction, a problem, and an outcome
- Has a problem specifically related to the weakness of the character
- Teaches a lesson about life
- Ends with a moral that summarizes the lesson

Standards Fables Support

Like other styles of narrative writing, fables support many of the NCTE/IRA standards described in the Introduction to Expressive Writing. Additionally, in learning about fables, students will learn about matching a moral to a story.

Lesson Plan Example: Fables

Activity Objectives

In this lesson, students will

- Compare the essential elements of fables with other narrative writings
- Pre-write in anticipation of writing a fable
- Write their own fables

Activity Summary

Students will consider the essential elements of fables and will listen to a reading of "The Lion and the Mouse." Students will then construct a pre-write for "The Lion and the Mouse" in preparation for creating pre-writes for their own fables. Each student will select a moral as the basis of his or her fable and begin to pre-write. When they have completed their pre-writing, the students will write their own fables.

Materials

- Overhead projector and transparencies
- Sample fables (see the end of this lesson)
- Pre-write handout
- Sample filled-out pre-write handout
- A copy of "The Lion and the Mouse" from *Aesop's Fables* (I recommend the translation by Jerry Pinkney.)

Description of Activities

1. Statement of Objectives

   - "Today we are going to discuss fables. I am going to read a fable to you from the book titled *Aesop's Fables,* and then we will complete a pre-writing activity that will help you organize your thoughts on what you want your own fable to be about."

2. Class Discussion

   - "Has anyone heard of a fable?" Discuss the students' responses, if any. "Although fables are very old, they are as popular today as they were thousands of years ago."

   - "Like other forms of expressive writing, fables have certain characteristics that make them unique." Discuss the essential elements of a fable with the class. A fable:

     Is a brief, fanciful tale

     Has characters, often including animals that act or talk like people (personification)

Has an introduction, a problem, and an outcome

Has a problem specifically related to the weakness of the character

Teaches a lesson about life

Ends with a moral that summarizes the lesson

- "Now that you understand the elements that make up a fable, I am going to read a fable to you today." Talk briefly about Aesop. "This book consists of sixty-eight of Aesop's fables, but he has written many, many more. All of these fables are well over 2,500 years old."

- Read aloud "The Lion and the Mouse."

3. Group Activity

- Ask students about the fable and the meaning of the moral: *even the strongest can sometimes use the help of the smallest.* "Are all the essential elements we discussed represented in this fable?"

- "As with our earlier narrative writings, a pre-write makes writing a fable much easier to do. Let's do a pre-write for the fable we just heard, so you can see how it's done." Construct a pre-writing example with the class for "The Lion and the Mouse" so they will understand how to complete their own pre-write.

4. Individual Activity

- "Now I will give you a list of some commonly heard morals, which you may use to help you write an outline for your fable. If you can think of a different moral, you may use your own." Distribute the list of morals.

- Briefly discuss some of the most common morals to ensure that students understand them.

- "Choose one of the morals on the list and think about a fable that would illustrate that moral. I will give you a blank pre-writing form for you to use in outlining your fable. If you have trouble thinking of an idea for a fable, raise your hand." Distribute the pre-writing worksheet for fables and the sample filled-in worksheet to serve as an example.

5. Closure

- "Does anyone have any questions so far, or are you confused about anything we have discussed?" Answer any questions that the students may have. "You will be using what you pre-write next time we meet to help you begin the first draft of your fable. If you are having trouble coming up with some ideas, think about it until our next lesson on fables."

Narrative Writing Example: **Fable 1**

The Queen of the Barn

A beautiful poodle named Prissy lived with several other dogs and cats on a farm. She was a very fancy dog. Her hobbies included brushing her hair, putting on make-up, and looking beautiful. She was like the queen of the farm. All of the other animals adored Prissy. A quiet rabbit named Holly, who was nowhere near as attractive as Prissy, didn't get much attention from the other animals. Her fur was mangled and her teeth stuck out, and none of the animals knew she had a good heart.

Whatever Prissy wanted, the other animals would get for her. "My, it's hot!" she would say, and the horse would run to get her a fan. "I sure am thirsty!" she would say, and a cat would run to fetch some water.

One cold winter day, a blizzard was rolling into the area. The animals were rushing to get all of the food into the barn, round up everyone so they wouldn't freeze to death, and collect the materials to make a fire. Even though they asked Prissy to help, she just sat at the front of the barn watching everyone work. "Why should I have to help you? You can do it," she exclaimed.

Meanwhile, Holly was working hard to get all of the food in. She was tiny, but she pushed and pulled with all her might. As the storm began to roar, a squirrel mother noticed that one of her babies was missing. Most of the animals were too afraid of the blizzard, but Holly went out into the storm, found the baby squirrel, and brought her back into the warm, dry barn.

The other animals cheered for Holly, except one.

"Big deal!" Prissy said. "I could have done that also."

At this point, the animals lost patience with Prissy's arrogant attitude. They sent her out into the storm, since she thought it was so easy. After a while, they let her back in so that she could get warm, but they all turned their backs on her, and she was all alone.

After that day, Holly became the queen of the barn, but she worked just as hard as anyone else, and the other animals appreciated her even more for that.

Moral: Beauty is only skin deep. Look deep inside someone to find the person that he or she truly is.

Narrative Writing Example: **Fable 2**

The Sloth Sisters

There once were two teenage sisters named Messhilda and Detra. Messhilda and Detra were both very smart and pretty girls who spent most of their time at home talking to their friends on the phone or using the computer. They shared a bedroom and a bathroom, and neither one had any desire to pick up after herself. Every day was a battle with their mom or dad about cleaning their room or bathroom. In their opinion, their parents made way too much of a big deal about it anyway, and they had more important things to worry about, such as boys, music, and clothes.

After much turmoil, their mom and dad decided to let the girls live as they desired in their own room and bathroom. They never said another word, and just waited to see what would happen. The girls hardly seemed to notice that their parents weren't pestering them anymore about cleaning up. They no longer bothered to pick up any clothes or towels or food, or clean either room whatsoever. They were happy in their private, messy space.

One day Messhilda and Detra decided to have a party. They made colorful flyers and invited all their best friends and were especially excited that their two boyfriends, Trod Nokiss and Aussome Shoveldirt, were coming. It was going to be a great party.

On the night of the party, tons of kids came and there was lots of fun being had. After a couple of hours of pizza and soda, Trod needed to go to the bathroom. He went down the hall and opened a door, hoping it was the bathroom. It was very dark, so he crept in and tried to find the light switch. All of a sudden, he found himself entangled in a web of clothes and other unidentifiable stuff. He panicked, and the more he struggled, the more he became entangled. He tried to yell for help but somehow a dirty sock became lodged in his mouth and he couldn't talk. He tried to find a way out, but was soon completely confused about where the door might be.

Aussome also went off to find the bathroom. He was luckier than Trod; the first door he tried was the right one. He went in and turned on the light and found himself surrounded by piles of dirty clothes, towels, and feminine objects that he found too horrible to describe. Trying to get out, he tripped over a pile of trash and fell to the floor. He tried to stand up, but became stuck to some sticky stuff. He was too horrified to even think what it could be. The odor in the room was pretty intense, and he soon passed out.

Soon after, the sisters and other kids wondered where Trod and Aussome were. Messhilda and Detra started to worry that they may have tried to go into their bedroom or bathroom. The search began. After a few hours without any luck in finding the lost boys, the Greater Smokey Mountain Search and Rescue team was brought in. Swiss Mountain dogs were also brought in to help. After a three-day search, Trod was found under a mound of dirty clothes in the corner of the girls' bedroom, scared and speechless. He had survived on some old pizza that he found on the floor.

Aussome was not as lucky. He was found a week later and needed serious medical attention due to dehydration, starvation, and mysterious sticky stuff on his body. Neither boy ever called Messhilda or Detra again.

Moral: Cleanliness is next to Godliness. No one likes to be around an extremely messy or slovenly person. Clean up after yourself for your benefit and that of your family and friends.

Narrative Writing Example: **Fable 3**

The Devoted Stud

Once upon a time, a beautiful young mare named Penny lived in a small town by the sea. There were many mares in this small town, but Penny was by far the most beautiful. Penny was always searching for a stud who would be completely and totally devoted to her and her alone.

Of the many eligible studs around the town, none fit her fancy. They all tried to win her over by bringing her sugar cubes or fresh alfalfa hay, but she wanted more. One stud, Merle, tried every day to win her over with little things, but to his dismay, Merle was unable to win her love. Every time Merle asked, "What is it about me that you will not marry me?" Penny would answer quaintly and to the point, "You have to *earn* my love."

Every day Merle continued to bring roses and poems, trying to win Penny's love. All attempts were in vain. Everyone in town thought Merle was crazy to continue chasing after her, but he would simply repeat what she said to him: "I have to *earn* her love."

One day Merle was walking over to Penny's pasture with a rose and a poem that he was especially proud of when he heard a loud "NNNEEEEEEEYYYY!!!" Something was wrong; worse, it sounded like his beloved Penny's voice. Merle dropped the poem and roses and ran as fast as he could to where the noise had originated. To his surprise, he found Penny in the river, pinned against a rock and the rushing current. If Merle didn't act quickly, she would be swept under and drown.

Merle hollered to Penny to hold on. He ran to the bank near where she was stuck, and with all his might he pushed against a tree that fell just to the side of Penny. Merle instructed her to grab the end closest to her and then he would pull the other end away from the river. With his strength and quick thinking, Merle was able to save Penny from a watery grave and earned her love forever.

Moral: A penny saved is a penny earned.

Pre-Writing Sample Worksheet: Fables

Fable Title: <u>The Queen of the Barn</u>

Animal Characters: <u>Prissy, a poodle</u>

<u>Holly, a rabbit</u>

<u>Other barn animals</u>

Human Characteristics: <u>Dog brushes her hair, puts on make-up, and talks</u>

<u>Animals do all of daily chores themselves</u>

<u>Fetch water for Prissy, get a fan for Prissy</u>

<u>Rescue other animals</u>

<u>Build a fire</u>

Problem: <u>Prissy will not pull her share of work around the barn, but everyone loves</u>

<u>her anyway.</u>

<u>Holly works hard, but is not attractive so no one notices her.</u>

<u>There is a storm coming and Prissy will not help out.</u>

<u>A baby squirrel is lost in the blizzard.</u>

Resolution: <u>Prissy makes a sassy remark and the other animals kick her out of</u>

<u>the barn into the cold.</u>

<u>Holly rescues the baby squirrel.</u>

<u>The animals appreciate her hard work.</u>

Moral: <u>Beauty is only skin deep.</u>

<u>Look deep inside someone to find out their true character.</u>

Name _____   Date _____

Pre-Writing Worksheet: Fables

Fable Title: _____

_____

Animal Characters: _____

_____

_____

_____

Human Characteristics: _____

_____

_____

_____

_____

Problem: _____

_____

_____

_____

_____

Resolution: _____

_____

_____

_____

_____

Moral: _____

_____

_____

_____

_____

FAIRY TALES

In the land of make-believe, anything can happen! Fairy tales help us believe just that. They also assist students in delving into their imagination. Fairy tales are short stories with love and adventure in them. They also include a magical event that is a key element in the story, which builds around characters that can include royalty and animals. In addition, fairy tales feature a hero or heroine and a villain.

Children love magical-mystical happenings. Some will be able to make connections in their own lives with that of the fairy tale.

Essential Elements

A fairy tale

- Is a short story that involves love and/or adventure
- Has a first sentence that identifies it (example: "Once upon a time . . .")
- Includes a magical event as a key element in the story
- Includes a hero/heroine and a villain
- Often includes royalty and animals
- Ends happily (example: ". . . happily ever after")

Standards Fairy Tales Support

Like other forms of narrative writing, fairy tales support many of the NCTE/IRA standards as described in the Introduction to Expressive Writing. Furthermore, in learning about fairy tales, students will appreciate the value of magic in storytelling. They will learn how to introduce elements of conflict and to bring a difficult story to a happy resolution.

Lesson Plan Example: Fairy Tales

Activity Objectives

In this lesson, students will

- Read a fairy tale, such as "The True Story of the Three Little Pigs"
- Identify the essential elements of a fairy tale
- Write their own fairy tales

Activity Summary

The students will listen to a reading of "The True Story of the Three Little Pigs." The students will then consider the essential elements of fairy tales. They will choose a topic for a fairy tale and then write their own fairy tales. Students will make a story book from all the fairy tales in the class.

Materials
- "The True Story of the Three Little Pigs" by Jon Scieska
- Sample fairy tales (see the end of this lesson)

Description of Activity
1. Statement of Objectives
   - "Today you will read a fairy tale, 'The True Story of the Three Little Pigs.' You will also identify the characteristics of a fairy tale. Then you will be ready to write your own fairy tale."
2. Class Discussion
   - "How many of you have ever read or heard the story called 'The Three Little Pigs'? Or what about 'Snow White'? These stories are called fairy tales, and today we are going to learn about fairy tales and even write one of our own."
   - "There are certain essential elements that make a story a fairy tale. Fairy tales are short stories that:

     Have a first sentence that always begins with 'Once upon a time . . .' and an ending that says 'happily ever after'

     Involve love or adventure

     Have something magical happen that is an important part of the story

     Have a hero or heroine and a villain

     Usually have royalty or animals in them"

- "Does anyone know what a villain is? A villain is the bad person in a story. Does everyone know what royalty means? Royalty means a king, queen, or other member of a monarch's family."

- "Today we are going to read together 'The True Story of the Three Little Pigs.'" Read the fairy tale to the class or have several students take turns reading portions of the story to their classmates.

- "Let's review the characteristics of a fairy tale, so that we can see whether or not the story we just heard was a fairy tale." Have students list the elements in this and other stories that make it a fairy tale.

- "Next you'll be writing your own fairy tale. So let's hear some ideas about some good fairy tale stories." Help the students to brainstorm some ideas to get them started on their own fairy tales. Put their list on the board, along with some ideas of your own.

3. Group Activity

   - "Let's review the important characteristics of a fairy tale." Ask students as a whole class to identify the elements of a fairy tale. "Now select a topic for your fairy tale." Help those students who cannot decide on a topic to select one.

4. Individual Activity

   - "When you have chosen a topic, begin to write your fairy tale. You'll start your writing in class and you will finish it for homework."

5. Closure

   - "Today we read a fairy tale and identified what elements make up a fairy tale. We also started on our very own fairy tales that will be put in a book that includes everyone's fairy tales. Tomorrow we are going to read another fairy tale and also look over the fairy tales we have written."

Narrative Writing Example: **Fairy Tale 1**

Leona and the Lizard

Once upon a time in a land far away there lived a young girl named Leona. Leona lived with her mother and father in a little cabin in the woods. Leona did not see much of the outside world. She enjoyed just being with her mother and father. She would spend her days helping her mother clean the house and cook and helping her father chop wood so that he could take it to a nearby town to sell.

Although Leona was very content with her life, one thing was missing. She wanted desperately to fall in love with a nice young man and live with him beside her parents in the woods. There was just one problem. Leona was a beautiful girl inside and out, but when she smiled, her teeth were so crooked that no one would have anything to do with her. She was teased whenever she went into the town.

Her parents showed her unconditional love, and this is why she wanted to live near them for the rest of her life. The local dentist in town had the ability to fix Leona's teeth, but he wouldn't because he was very jealous of Leona's beauty. He knew that if he fixed her teeth, his daughter Sarah would no longer be the most beautiful maiden in the town. Every night, Leona pleaded privately for her dreams to come true. She was sure that, if her teeth were fixed, she could meet and marry the man of her dreams.

Then one night, a magical lizard, Pedro, came to Leona and told her that she would meet a man the next day in the forest. He would tempt her to run away with him and never see her family again. Pedro warned Leona against being enticed by this man. Pedro said that the man's promises were an evil trick arranged by the dentist to remove Leona forever. Pedro promised that if Leona did the right thing, good things would come to her. The next day, Leona was walking in the woods when she came across a handsome man. He told her how awed he was by her beauty and asked her to run away with him. Leona was very tempted. She had always wanted to fall in love, and now was her perfect chance.

Despite how much she wanted to follow the stranger, she considered Pedro's advice and sent the handsome man on his way. Then she sat down by a tree and began to cry. What if this was her only chance at love? Suddenly, Pedro appeared. He thanked her for taking his advice. One of Leona's tears fell onto Pedro. Suddenly, he turned into a handsome young prince. He told Leona that she was the only one who had respected him. An evil witch had cast him out of his kingdom and turned him into a lizard. The only way he could become a human again was for someone to respect him even as a lizard. Pedro didn't mind her crooked teeth, but he knew Leona was very unhappy. He arranged for Leona's teeth to be magically fixed, and the two were married at once. The prince moved Leona's parents to a beautiful house near the castle, so they lived happily ever after beside Leona's parents.

Narrative Writing Example: **Fairy Tale 2**

Sabrina and the Prince

Once upon a time in a land not far away lived a beautiful girl named Sabrina. Sabrina lived with her very evil aunt and wickedly mean cousin named Mary. Sabrina's parents had died when she was very young. Sabrina didn't enjoy life with her new family. Her aunt made her do all of the housework and would not allow her to go anywhere, unless it was for the aunt's or Mary's benefit. Mary and her mother certainly didn't want Sabrina to meet a gentleman, because then who would do all the work?

Mary was always with her friends, although she did not have many because she was so mean, but Sabrina had to stay home and clean. Sabrina dreamed a great deal about meeting a man and falling in love and getting married, but she also dreamed about seeing her parents again.

Sometimes at night Sabrina would sneak out for a late night walk while her aunt and cousin were sleeping. One night as Sabrina was out walking, she sat down and cried until her tears formed a puddle. And there in the puddle she saw her parents' faces. She cried out to them, and they assured her that everything would be okay. Sabrina did not want to leave because it had been so long since she had seen her parents.

After talking with them, she decided to go home because sunrise was approaching and she did not want her aunt to realize she had been gone. If the aunt knew that Sabrina had been gone, she would lock Sabrina up at night.

The next night Sabrina went out again. She cried, in the hopes that she could make a puddle and see her parents, and it worked. Her parents had come up with a plan. They told her that on the following day she should leave to fetch water for her aunt, but this time a prince would be waiting to take her away.

Sabrina's parents, although they were dead, had arranged for a king and queen from another country not too far away to hear how Sabrina was being treated. Sabrina's parents told the king and queen that Sabrina would be at the river the following day. They asked their son, the prince, to do something about it. They also told the prince how beautiful Sabrina was.

The prince arrived early in the morning so he would be sure not to miss seeing her. That afternoon Sabrina showed up, and the prince approached her. He spoke to her about her parents and she knew that he was safe to be with. He took her back to his palace, where she was treated very nicely. On the first anniversary of her parents' death, she married the prince. Sabrina and the prince, together, lived happily ever after.

SPOOKY STORIES

Telling ghost stories is part of being a child. Building on the concept takes students into narrative writing in a new way. Spooky stories include the same guidelines as a short story, with a twist on the theme of the story.

Students quickly respond with excitement about writing spooky stories. However, as the teacher, you must set guidelines from the start. Explain to the students that in their ghost stories, (1) no one gets hurt, (2) no weapons are used, and (3) no one is threatened. The ghost stories written with these guidelines will be deliciously spooky but not gruesome.

Essential Elements

Spooky stories

- Have an introduction that grabs the reader's attention, establishes a setting, and introduces the main character
- Have an interesting conflict that heightens interest as the plot develops
- Have a conflict that falls into one of three categories: character versus character, character versus self, or character versus nature
- Include a single event called the climax, which is the peak of the interest level
- End with a conclusion that includes resolution of the conflict
- Often have a fall/seasonal setting
- Have a spooky or mysterious element (scary but not dangerous)

For this lesson, our spooky stories will NOT include

- Violence or weapons
- Blood or gore
- Anyone being killed

Standards Spooky Stories Support

Writing spooky stories supports many of the NCTE/IRA standards as described in the Introduction to Expressive Writing.

Students will learn the elements of a spooky story and how to pace a story in order to scare the reader in a safe, non-threatening way.

Lesson Plan Example: Spooky Stories

Activity Objectives

In this lesson, students will

- Listen to a spooky story, "There's a Nightmare in My Closet" by Mercer Mayer
- Consider the essential elements of a spooky story
- Discuss the specialized vocabulary required for writing a spooky story
- Choose a topic for a spooky story, and then write their own spooky stories

Activity Summary

Students will listen to a spooky story, "There's a Nightmare in My Closet" by Mercer Mayer. Students will consider the essential elements of a spooky story and will discuss the specialized vocabulary needed to make a story mysterious and suspenseful. Students will then choose topics for their own spooky stories and will write their own spooky stories.

Materials
- A copy of "There's a Nightmare in My Closet" by Mercer Mayer
- Examples of spooky stories (see end of this lesson)
- Essential elements of spooky stories on a transparency
- Selected spooky passages on transparencies (selected by the teacher)
- Overhead projector
- Writing paper and pens
- CD player and some age-appropriate creepy music

Description of Activities
1. Statement of Objectives
   - "Today we are going to learn what it takes to make a spooky story, and then you will write one of your own."

2. Class Discussion

   - Get the students' attention by turning out the lights and playing age-appropriate creepy music.

   - Read "There's a Nightmare in My Closet" by Mercer Mayer. At various points, stop reading and have the students predict and explain what they think will happen next in the story. At the end of the story, ask questions such as, "How did this story feel?" or "What makes this story spooky—but not scary?"

   - Place a transparency of the essential elements of spooky stories on the overhead projector. Explain the requirements of a spooky story to the students. Spooky stories:

     Have an introduction that grabs the reader's attention, establishes a setting, and introduces the main character

     Have an interesting conflict that heightens interest as the plot develops

     Have a conflict that falls into one of three categories: character versus character, character versus self, or character versus nature

     Include a single event called the climax, which is the peak of the interest level

     End with a conclusion that includes resolution of the conflict

     Often have a fall/seasonal setting

     Have a spooky or mysterious element (scary but not dangerous)

   - Use "There's a Nightmare in My Closet" to illustrate these requirements and restrictions. For example, the story contains no violence, no weapons, no blood and gore, and no one is killed. These stories are spooky, but not dangerous. Ask the students, "Did any of this occur in our story?" Emphasize that the boy in the story was never in danger, yet the story had enough mystery that no one knew for sure that he was not going to get hurt until the end.

   - Explain to the students that spooky story writing is basically the same as other forms of narrative writing, and say that they need to include all of the same elements, such as use of transitions from one paragraph to the next paragraph. Explain: "But spooky stories, by their nature, require a different vocabulary than other narrative writings use. Spooky stories require spooky descriptive words to create the proper mood." Display transparencies with some sample writing to show students words that may help create the spooky effects. Have the students suggest some effective words for a spooky story; write the best suggestions on the board.

3. Group Activity

   - Group the students into pairs so that they can generate ideas for their stories. "Now it's time for you to write your own spooky stories. Use everything that you've learned so far about expressive narrative writing to create a *really* spooky story."

- Have each student select a topic for his or her spooky story and begin writing. Guide the students as they work on their stories, answering and explaining anything that they might not have understood.

4. Individual Activity

- Give the students some time to finish their stories on their own. Move from student to student to see how they are coming along with their writing.

5. Closure

- "Well class, you did a wonderful job on your spooky stories. Today you learned what the elements of a spooky story are and how to write one of your own."

- Have them go home and have their parents help them to edit their work and to create a picture and glue the picture and the corrected story on a sheet of black or orange construction paper. You might suggest that the finished projects be posted on the bulletin board during the week of Halloween.

Sample Narrative Writing: **Spooky Story 1**

Ghosts Need Friends Too

It was the night before Halloween and Pat, Charlie, Jack, and Daniel decided to hang out and play a game of hide-and-go-seek. The night was mysterious. All four of them felt as if a fifth person had somehow joined them, but no one said anything. As they played, they kept hearing loud footsteps behind them, but when they stopped or turned around the footsteps stopped. If they were laughing and they stopped, the laughing would seem to continue for a few seconds. The four of them ignored all the strange signs and decided to start their game of hide-and-go-seek.

Pat was chosen to be "it" first, so he leaned against the tree and put his head in the crook of his arm and started to count to thirty. Charlie, Jack, and Daniel took off to hide.

Charlie hid under the deck in the back of the house. He thought he saw something out of the corner of his eye and turned to look, but when he turned around it was gone. When Pat finished counting and went to look for his friends, suddenly he heard a soft voice whisper to him, "Look under the deck."

Pat looked around to see who had whispered, but there was nobody there. But he went to look under the deck. There he found Charlie and yelled, "You're it!" Charlie crawled out in disbelief; he thought Pat must have cheated. As Jack and Daniel came out, they thought so, too.

After this, Charlie went to count while the other boys went to hide. Jack and Daniel were hiding together, and they too thought they kept seeing someone but never got a good view of who it might be. Pat hid behind the storage building, and as he stood there he began to wonder, "Who told me where Charlie was hiding?"

He didn't think he'd spoken aloud, but he got an answer. "It was me," a soft voice whispered. Pat turned and there sat a glowing figure of a small boy. Pat jumped back in shock, but was not really scared because the boy looked harmless.

Pat asked, "Were you the one who told me where Charlie was?"

The little boy said, "Yes, I was." Pat could see he was a ghost, and he started asking him all sorts of questions, and even tried to touch him—but of course you can't touch ghosts. The ghost's name was Richard and he was thirteen, just about the same age as the boys.

When Pat heard the other boys come looking for him, he came out of hiding and told the boys that he had someone that he wanted them to meet. He warned them not to be afraid. When he introduced the other boys to Richard, Jack and Daniel got up and ran, scared to death. Charlie, feeling a little braver, stayed to see how things went. However, curiosity soon got the best of Jack and Daniel, and slowly they crept back. Pat, Charlie, and Richard watched as the runaway boys peeked around the corner of a nearby building. Pat assured them that it was safe, and they came over and introduced themselves. They all wanted to know what it was like to be a ghost, and Richard was eager to answer. All Richard had ever wanted was a friend, and now he had four.

Narrative Writing Example: **Spooky Story 2**

Warning

Rain poured down in drenching bucketfuls, and icy blasts of water whipped at Katherine, chilling her to the bone. The wind made an almost animal-like howling sound as it ripped through the trees, bending the cedars first one way then another. Katherine was out on this dreadful, moonless night, alone and terrified. She was running almost blindly through the darkness, searching frantically for someone to help her.

Until today, Katherine had always been a cheerful, happy-go-lucky teenager. She was never one to worry about anything. If you had asked her before this night, she would have been the first to tell you that she led a charmed life. She was invincible; nothing bad ever happened to her and it never would.

Now she knew better. Life could change so much in just a few short minutes from making just one tiny decision. Katherine had received a warning a short time earlier, but she ignored it. It was so like her to brush it off. She remembered now how carelessly she had laughed and continued on her merry way, unaware of what lay in store. In Katherine's sheltered, happy little world, bad things only happened to other people. Now she was paying the price for ignoring that earlier cautionary plea. Oh, why hadn't she listened? Why had she put herself in danger? She was on her own now, suffering the consequences of her choice.

In order to fight off the fear, Katherine allowed herself to feel anger. She was furious with herself, and she mentally gave herself a kick. She relived the last few minutes. It had happened like a slow-moving nightmare, where she was unable to do anything but watch helplessly. She just had time to grab her cell phone before she got out and began to run at full speed. Then in horror she realized the call she made for help was not going through. She looked at her phone to see what was wrong. The blue glowing panel simply said "dead zone." Katherine gulped. She was already frightened enough and hoped that this was not a foreshadowing of what was to come.

The lighted message spurred Katherine on as she tore through the night, drenched to the skin. She stopped and tried to look around. She had the feeling she had lost her bearings. Was she even going in the right direction for help? she wondered. A streak of lightning flashed nearby and the sound of thunder came immediately with it. The brunt of the storm was now fully upon her. She looked about wildly.

As best she could make out through the heavy sheets of rain, she saw what appeared to be an old, weatherworn house in the distance. It was at the end of a dirt road. One lone candle flickered menacingly in the window. Whose house was it? Why were their lights off on a night like this? Katherine hesitated. Another big bolt of lightning struck nearby, and that was all she needed to help make up her mind. She headed to the flickering light.

Katherine stepped quietly onto the porch, thankful for the shelter from the rain. She shook her drenched clothes and gave her soggy hair a squeeze. She tried to peer through the murky front window, but could see nothing. Katherine stood as straight and tall as she possibly could to bolster her confidence. Her hand raised and she bravely knocked on the old wooden door.

Faces appeared in the window, peering at her. Before she knew what was happening, the door creaked open and at least two pairs of firm hands were pulling her in. What had she gotten herself into now?

"Land sakes!" the elderly couple declared. "Katherine, what on earth are you doing out in this weather, in the middle of the night? It's not fit for man or beast."

"Earl," the old woman spoke sharply to her husband. "You run and grab a towel and bring back a blanket too while you're at it. Katherine, honey, you come on over here and warm up by the fireplace while I go get you a cup of hot cocoa."

Katherine finally found her voice. "Thank you, Mrs. Kramer." A few minutes later, she was toweling herself dry, then wrapped up tightly in the toasty comforter. "I thought your house was somewhere around here, but I got turned around in the storm and wasn't quite sure," said Katherine.

Myrtle Kramer held the cup of hot chocolate over the open fireplace, trying to heat it up for her friend's granddaughter. "That storm knocked out our electricity," she explained, "but this will heat up quickly enough over the flame. Now, tell us, what on earth is going on?"

Katherine laughed. "I've just got one thing to say," she told the Kramers. "The next time you are out for a drive and your low fuel warning light comes on, don't ignore it!"

AUTOBIOGRAPHICAL INCIDENTS

The autobiographical incident is a well-told story about a specific occurrence in a writer's life. It uses vivid sensory details to engage the reader in the event. It also includes some kind of revelation, implied or stated, about the event's significance to the writer. The author's voice is natural and honest, allowing the reader to experience and share the feelings of the author during the event.

Essential Elements

An autobiographical incident

- Describes a single event in the first person
- Describes the event in sequential order (beginning, middle, and end)
- Incorporates vivid descriptions and sensory details

Standards Autobiographical Incidents Support

Like other forms of narrative writing, autobiographical incidents support many of the NCTE/IRA standards as described in the Introduction to Expressive Writing.

Students will learn to tell a story from their lives in an interesting fashion. This creative process will enable all students to gain new insights about their lives and learn that their lives can be interesting to other people.

Lesson Plan Example: Autobiographical Incidents (Part 1)

Activity Objectives

In this lesson, students will

- Consider the essential elements used in writing a narrative about an autobiographical incident

- Examine their own lives for interesting situations suitable for an expressive narrative
- Create a pre-write in preparation for writing about an autobiographical incident

Activity Summary

Students will consider the essential elements of an autobiographical incident. Each student will then select an incident from his or her own life and create a pre-write on that incident.

Materials

- Autobiographical incident pre-writing example on a transparency (see end of this lesson)
- Autobiographical incident pre-writing template on a transparency (see end of this lesson)
- Overhead projector

Description of Activities

1. Statement of Objectives
   - "Our topic today is an autobiographical incident. Today we will be writing about something that is close to you all. Yourselves! We will be discussing an autobiographical incident, which is a story that describes an event in the life of the actual writer of the story, told in the 'first person.' Then each one of you will write about an event in your life from the past or present."

2. Class Discussion
   - "Last time we discussed spooky stories and you had a great time writing your own spooky tales. You all did a wonderful job writing your stories and using your imaginations. Now we're going to try writing something new. Before we get into that, can anyone tell me what 'first person' means?" Guide the students into a discussion of the differences between writing in the first person (I, me, we), second person (you), and third person (he, she, they).
   - "An autobiographical incident is a story that you write about *you*. It describes a single event and should be written in sequential order." Review the three parts of a narrative: beginning, middle, and end. "Of course, your story should incorporate vivid descriptions and sensory details. Each of you has lots of stories to tell, and this is your opportunity to write about yourselves."

3. Group Activity
   - "Before you write your own stories, we'll go through pre-writing details. On the overhead, I have placed a sample autobiographical incident and

its pre-write. The first pre-written activity is the *main event*." Point out the main event on the sample pre-write.

- "Second, I want you to describe the setting. Whatever you write about, I want you to include where it took place." Point out the setting description on the pre-write.

- "Next, and this is the bulk of the pre-write, is the events chart. I want you to write four to five events leading up to your story." Show the students the events chart. "To the side, I want you to write your sensory details, such as scared, nervous, happy, or sad."

- "Last, I want you to include a conclusion at the end. This will be the last line of your writing and where you 'wrap up' your autobiographical incident."

- "Now it's time for you to start your own autobiographical incident. Let's begin by making a chart similar to the example. I want you to place your main event, setting, the events chart, and the conclusion of events in sequence. Next, I want you to brainstorm ideas about your autobiography. Remember, the more detail you have, the easier it will be to tell your story.

4. Individual Activity

- Hand out blank pre-writing forms for an autobiographical incident. "Now it's time to begin. I want you to take this time to carefully fill in the chart like the one we just made. Do not rush to finish your story because this assignment is about the pre-writing only! Make the pre-writing outline as thorough as possible and give me some interesting details. As always, if you need help, do not hesitate to ask."

5. Closure

- "Today class, we have discussed the autobiographical incident and the pre-write that is needed to assist in the writing. When you are finished with the pre-write, I will gather them up and in our next lesson, you will use them to write your final paper."

Lesson Plan Example: Autobiographical Incidents (Part 2)

Activity Objectives

In this lesson, students will

- Review the essential elements of an autobiographical incident
- Use their pre-written examples to develop autobiographical incident narratives

Activity Summary

The students will review the Autobiographical Incident Preparation handout. The students will then use what they pre-wrote earlier to write autobiographical incidents of their own. When they complete their autobiographical incidents, students will share their efforts with the rest of the class.

Materials

- Example of an autobiographical incident and its pre-write as transparencies (see end of this lesson)
- Autobiographical Incident Preparation handout (see end of this lesson)
- An overhead projector

Description of Activities

1. Statement of Objectives
   - "Today you will write up the autobiographical incident you started during the last lesson, being sure to give your personal story in full detail. You will take the information from the pre-write you did and make a formal narrative."

2. Class Discussion
   - "During our last lesson, you all did some pre-work on autobiographical incidents from your own lives. Today, you will use that work and turn it into a narrative. The fact that you have done some pre-writing will make it that much easier to write your stories."
   - "As you see on this sample autobiographical incident, we have an introduction, a body, and a conclusion." Point out these portions of the sample narrative.
   - Now show the pre-write sample and explain how the author constructed a narrative from it. Answer any questions.
   - "We will now review the essential elements needed to make your formal narrative."

3. Group Activity
   - "The way you write an autobiographical incident is different from how you would write a spooky story or a fable. Let's consider some of the differences." Distribute the Autobiographical Incident Preparation handout and lead a group discussion on the different topics.

4. Individual Activity

- "Now it is time to do *your* writing. I want each of you to place a title at the top of your paper. Make it as creative as possible. Pay close attention to details and use as many sensory words as you possibly can. Let's begin."

- "As with all the other lessons that I have assigned, I am expecting great results on your autobiographical sketch." Tell the students to do rough drafts of their stories first. Then they will edit and revise them. "When you are finished writing your rough draft, hand it in to me. If you have any questions, raise your hand." Leave the example on the overhead to assist the children if needed.

5. Closure

- "Today (as well as during the last class) we have learned the essential elements of an autobiographical incident. We have learned that it is an event in the first person and it uses vivid descriptions and details. Along with the actual story, we have also done a pre-write to assist in the process. You have been very patient and I thank you for all the attention you have given me." If time permits, have students share some of their stories with the class.

Autobiographical Incident Preparation

When writing about an autobiographical incident, the writer narrates a coherent and engaging story that moves the narrative toward the central moment. The narrative tells readers what they need to know to understand what happens and to infer its significance to the writer. The following strategies will help to make an autobiographical incident interesting:

- Naming (specific names of people or objects, quantities, numbers)

- Describing visual details of scenes, objects, or people (size, colors, shapes, features, dress)

- Describing sounds or smells or anything that appeals to the senses

- Narrating specific action (movements, gestures, postures, expressions)

- Creating dialogues, interior monologues, or expressing remembered feelings or insights at the time of the incident

- Slowing the pace to elaborate the central moment in the incident

- Creating suspense or tension

- Including the element of surprise

- Comparing or contrasting other scenes or people

    The writer should choose one experience that took place in his or her life and tell it in story form.

    The writer chooses the incident and tells it in a way that the reader can visualize the scene, the people, and the events. The writer should use carefully chosen details relevant to the incident, such as where the incident occurred, what people said, and how the writer felt. The writer should also include any background information necessary to understanding the relevance of the story.

    The essay reveals why the incident was important to the writer. This significance can be either implied or stated. The writer should let the reader know how the experience affected him or her, what he or she learned, or how he or she changed as a result. The reflections may be humorous.

    The writer should use an authentic voice that reveals the writer's attitude toward the incident. The essay should include well-chosen details; apt words; and graceful, varied sentences. It can also include word play and imagery. The essay should engage the reader from the start and move to a satisfying closure.

Name _____ Date _____

Pre-Writing Sample Worksheet:
Autobiographical Incidents

Main Event: going to Disney World

_____

_____

_____

_____

Setting: Orlando, Florida

_____

_____

_____

Event Chart:

Events	Sensory Details
got up early because we were staying 2 hours away	cold outside, very windy
car ride to Disney World	heat in the warm car/excitement
got to Disney World	bright and sunny, music playing
spent the day inside rides, smelled wonderful food, and shows	burgers, fries, cotton candy—still fairly cold
favorite ride	Space Mountain
Space Mountain	rode it 3 times, lots of flashing lights

Conclusion: Headed back to West Palm Beach that night very content and very tired. Could not stop talking about my day at Disney World.

_____

_____

Pre-Writing Sample Worksheet: Autobiographical Incidents

Main Event: _____

_____

_____

_____

Setting: _____

_____

_____

_____

Event Chart:

Events	Sensory Details
_____	_____
_____	_____
_____	_____
_____	_____
_____	_____
_____	_____
_____	_____
_____	_____

Conclusion: _____

_____

_____

_____

Narrative Writing Example: **Autobiographical Incident**

My Trip to Disney World

As I awoke from my bed and looked out the window, I was excited to see sunshine and blue skies. Today was going to be perfect. It was the perfect day to go to Disney World. I had been in West Palm Beach, Florida, for about four days with my parents and my two closest friends, Mark and Todd. I had always wanted to go to Disney World, and today we were finally going. "Wake up! Wake up!" I told the guys. I was ready to go. We all threw on our t-shirts and shorts, and we were soon out the door.

When I stepped outside, I felt a blast of cold air. It had to be 40 degrees, and here we were with t-shirts and shorts on. Oh well . . . I hoped it would warm up. The strong wind made the air feel even colder. We hopped in the back seat of the car, and my dad sped off. We were two hours away from Orlando and Disney World. The anticipation was killing me. I can still remember sitting in the warm, cozy car asking Mom and Dad, "Are we there yet? How much longer do we have?"

We finally pulled into the parking lot at Disney World. I was so excited I just couldn't stand it. It was bright and sunny and 65 degrees in Orlando. When I got out of the car, I heard "It's a Small World" playing. At the entrance gate were Goofy and Mickey there to greet everyone. Once we were inside, I didn't know where to start. I wanted to see and do everything. The food smelled wonderful. The smells of burgers, French fries, hot dogs, and cotton candy overwhelmed me. I wanted to eat, but we decided to ride some rides first. Todd and Mark knew it was my day, so they went along with all my choices.

We rode Splash Mountain, where we came plunging down into the cold water. On Big Thunder Mountain Railroad, we got to pretend we were on a runaway train in the mountains. I enjoyed climbing in the Swiss Family Robinson Tree House and riding on the Jungle Boat Cruise. My absolute favorite, however, was Space Mountain. This is an indoor roller coaster that you ride in the pitch dark. It makes you feel like you're zipping aimlessly through space. I rode this ride three times. After the third time, my parents said that it was time to go home. I looked up at Cinderella's castle shining brightly through the night and said goodbye to Disney World.

As we were heading back to West Palm Beach that night, I could not stop talking about my day at Disney World. While I was very tired from walking around all day, I'd had one of the best days that I could remember in a long time. I will never forget going to Disney World. I can't wait to go back!

PROMPTS

Personal Narrative Prompts

These personal narrative prompts are helpful in giving students ideas for themes for their own personal narratives. In each case, themes are listed first, followed by the actual prompts.

Themes

1. Receiving a substantial amount of money for the first time
2. Doing the right thing, when friends are doing the wrong thing
3. A time when you were really afraid
4. A special time with a friend
5. Earning money for a special "want"
6. Advice from an elder
7. Losing something special to you
8. A time that made you sad
9. Your favorite Christmas (or other family holiday)
10. Playing a game you enjoy
11. Choosing a weekly family outing
12. When you felt unappreciated
13. Helping someone learn something
14. Most recent visit to the dentist
15. Doing something special for someone
16. A school assignment you enjoyed
17. Completing a task
18. Annual family tradition
19. A special gift to surprise someone
20. Visit to an amusement park

Personal Narrative Prompts

1. Think about the first time you received what you considered to be a substantial amount of money; you may have received it as a gift or as payment

for a chore. Create a story telling about this event. Include such things as how you received the money, who gave it to you, and how it made you feel. Don't forget to include the events that happened before, during, and after the money was yours.

2. Think about a time when you were with your friends and they did something that they were not supposed to do. Instead of going along with your friends, you decided to do the right thing. Write a story about this event. As you plan your story, remember to tell about one particular event and focus on what happened before, during, and after the experience.

3. Think about a time when you were really afraid. Write a story about that time. Remember to include what happened to make you so afraid. Also include important facts, such as where this took place and how the event made you feel. Be sure to include a beginning, middle, and end.

4. Think about a time when you did something really special with a friend. Write a story telling about this event. As you write, remember to include information such as where and with whom this took place, why you felt this was special, how you felt as you experienced the event.

5. Think about a time in your past when you wanted something really badly, such as a special toy, recording of music, or an article of clothing. Your parents agreed you could have it, but insisted you had to earn your own money for it. Write a story telling how you earned the money for your purchase. Remember to include a beginning, middle, and ending to your story.

6. Think about advice an older person has given you in the past. It could be advice from a grandparent, parent, an aunt or uncle, or even an older brother or sister. Write a story about this advice. Include information such as what you thought of the advice, whether or not you accepted it, whether it worked, and how it made you feel knowing people cared enough to want to help you. Remember to focus on before you received the advice, during, and after the advice was given.

7. Think about a time when you lost something that was special to you. It could have been a favorite toy, article of clothing, or an item you collected. Write a story telling about this event. Remember to focus on only one item lost and tell what happened before, during, and after the incident.

8. Think about a time when you were sad. What happened in the course of events that made you feel that way? How did those feelings subside? Did anyone help you get over your feeling of sadness? Write a story about these events and who or what happened to help you overcome your feeling of sadness. Remember to tell about the events related to your feeling sad and be sure your story has a beginning, middle, and end.

9. Think about your favorite Christmas (or other family holiday) ever. What made this particular holiday so special? Was it because of a special gift you received, or perhaps a memory of a special family member or friend? Write a story about that particular day. Include specifics about why you recall it being so special.

10. Think about a time that you played a game you really enjoyed. You could have been playing alone, with a friend, or with a family member. Create a story telling about this game. As you write your paper, remember to describe the game you enjoyed and include a beginning, middle, and end.

11. Think about a time when you were allowed to choose a weekly family outing. Where did you choose to go, and what did you do as a family? Write a story that describes this event in words. Remember to focus on only one event and tell about what happened before, during, and after the event.

12. Think about a time when you felt unappreciated. It could have been the result of something that happened at home, school, or elsewhere. What caused you to feel this way? Who was involved? Do you think their intentions were deliberate? Write a story telling about that event. Remember to include events before, during, and after the incident.

13. Think about a time you helped someone learn to do something, such as play a new game or get through a tough problem. Write a story about that situation. What did you do? How did you help the other person? How did you feel afterward?

14. Think about your last visit to the dentist. It could have been for a regular check-up or to address a certain problem, such as having a cavity filled or a tooth pulled. Write a story about this particular visit. Remember to include details about before, during, and after the visit.

15. Think about a time when you did something special for someone. It could have been a friend, a family member, a neighbor, or someone you didn't know. Write a story about one time when you did something special or a time that someone did something special for you. Remember to tell about the events before, during, and after the act of kindness occurred.

16. Think about a school assignment that you thoroughly enjoyed. It could have been a project, report, or even a test. Write a story about the assignment. What was it? How did you accomplish it? Remember to include a beginning, middle, and end.

17. Think about a time that you completed a task that made you feel proud or happy. It could have been at home, at school, or at work. Write a story about this time. Remember to include background information about the task, why you were proud of completing it, and how it made you feel.

18. Think about a special tradition in your family that you celebrate only once a year. How do you and your family celebrate this event, and why is it special to you? Write a story about your special family tradition. Be sure your paper has a beginning, middle, and end.

19. Think about a time when you surprised someone with a special gift. It may have been a teacher, a family member, or a friend. Write a story telling about this event. As you write your paper, remember to tell about the events before, during, and after the incident.

20. Think about a time when you visited an amusement park with your family, friends, or classmates. Write a story telling about your trip. Remember to include details of the amusement park and tell about events at the beginning, middle, and end of the visit.

Imaginative Narrative Prompts

Imaginative narrative prompts are helpful to students by giving them ideas about imaginative incidents on which to base their narrative writings. Themes are listed first, followed by the actual prompts.

Themes
1. You are a famous musical artist.
2. You are a king/queen for a day.
3. Your hot air balloon goes down in the middle of the forest.
4. You have a magic mirror.
5. You have your own private island.
6. You hear a voice calling your name.
7. NASA wants to send you to Mars.
8. There is an alligator in your front yard.
9. You come upon a talking tree.
10. You explore a new planet.
11. Your toys come to life.
12. You are marooned on a deserted island.
13. You discover you can fly.
14. There is an alien in your house.
15. You are your favorite fairy tale character.
16. You win a day with your favorite star.
17. You wake up in a shopping mall after the stores are closed.
18. You are in the middle of a severe storm.
19. You find a treasure chest in your backyard.
20. You have an extra pair of arms and legs.
21. All technology stops working.
22. You are abducted by aliens.
23. You get off a bus in an unknown place.
24. You enter college as a freshman—but you are only 10 years old.
25. You're a character in a painting/photograph/image.

26. You wake up as an animal/object/gas.

27. You're a reporter covering the Revolutionary War.

28. You wake to the end of the world as you know it.

29. You are lost in the woods, and you are saved by the Three Bears.

30. You vacation in the Caribbean Islands on a magic carpet.

31. You are trapped under a fallen tree and must free yourself.

32. Write a story building on the end of a story you have read.

Imaginative Narrative Prompts

1. Imagine you are a famous musical artist. You can perform any style of music you wish. Write a story telling about how your "big break" into the music business occurred. Be sure that your story has a beginning, middle, and end.

2. Imagine you wake up one morning in a faraway land and you're told that you are the King or Queen of that land for the day. Tell a story about your experiences as leader of this faraway land. As you write your paper, remember to include a beginning, middle, and an end to your story.

3. Imagine you are on a hot air balloon ride on a sunny day and your balloon goes down in the middle of a mysterious forest. Write a story about your two-day stay in the forest before you are rescued. Remember to include events happening before, during, and after your balloon accident.

4. Imagine you have a magic mirror in your bedroom through which you (and only you) can pass in and out. Write a story about an adventure you had through the magic mirror. Remember to include descriptions of what you see and things you experience on your adventure.

5. Imagine you have been given your own private island. You can develop your island in any manner you wish. Tell about what you would like to build on the island and how the space on the island could be best used. Remember to include a beginning, middle, and end to your story.

6. Imagine you are sitting on your bed in your room and you hear a voice calling your name. The voice is coming from your closet. You open the door to your closet and find another door—a secret door. Write a story about what happens when you open that door and walk through it. Remember to focus on events before, during, and after your adventure takes place.

7. Imagine you are asked by NASA to visit the planet Mars. Write about what you think it will be like to visit Mars as you contemplate whether you will take NASA up on their offer. What issues would you have to consider before you agree to go? What will be your final decision?

8. Imagine you get off the school bus one afternoon and, as you approach the front of your yard, you see a large alligator on the sidewalk. Write a story about what you do to get past the alligator and into the house. Be sure your story has a beginning, middle, and end.

9. Suppose you are walking through a forest and you notice a strange tree. This strange tree begins to talk to you, telling you about hidden secrets of the forest. Write a story about what the tree tells you and your experience that follows as a result. Remember to include events before, during, and after the tree speaks to you.

10. Imagine NASA has discovered a new planet in our solar system and you have been chosen to join the team of astronauts who will explore this new planet. Write a story telling about your exploration. What is the planet like? What does it look like? What types of life forms do you find? Remember to include a beginning, middle, and end.

11. Imagine you are playing with your toys one afternoon and they come alive. Write a story about what happens after that. Remember to include a beginning, middle, and end.

12. Imagine that you have become marooned on a deserted island. Write a story about your experience being trapped on the island. Remember to include descriptions of what is on the island. Make sure your paper has a beginning, middle, and end.

13. Imagine you're walking down a flight of steps when suddenly you trip. Instead of falling down, you discover that you can fly. Write a story about what happens after that discovery. Remember to include a beginning, middle, and end.

14. Imagine one morning you wake up to find an alien in your house. The alien decides to spend the day with you. Write a story about what happens during the day. What does the alien look like? What do you do together? What does he eat for lunch? As you write your story, remember to include a beginning, middle, and end.

15. Imagine you are a character in your favorite fairy tale. What character are you? Write a story telling about your adventures as your chosen character. As you write, remember to include a beginning, middle, and end.

16. Imagine that one day you hear your name announced on your favorite radio station as winner of the "All-Star Contest." Your prize is an all expense-paid day with your favorite music, television, or sports star. Write a story telling about this wonderful adventure. As you write, remember to include information on events before, during, and after your special day.

17. Imagine you awake in the middle of the night to find yourself in a shopping mall. The only people there are you and your best friend. All the stores are closed. Write a story describing the night the mall belonged to you. Remember to include a beginning, middle, and end to the story.

18. Imagine that a severe storm has hit the area where you live. Tell what you experienced, what was damaged, and what was okay. As you write, remember to describe what happened that day, to provide specific details, and to present your ideas clearly. Be sure to include a beginning, middle, and end to your story.

19. Imagine that you and your best friend found a treasure chest. As you began to open the chest, a magic genie appeared. Write a story about what the genie said and what happened after that. Remember to include a beginning, middle, and end to the story.

20. Imagine you awoke one morning to find you had grown an extra pair of legs and arms during the night. Write a story telling what that was like. As you write, remember to include descriptions and focus on a beginning, middle, and end.

21. Imagine yourself in the year 2020, when suddenly all of the world's technologies stop working. You decide to publish a daily newspaper, and you make ten copies by hand. In this first story, describe a day in the life of someone in this new non-technological society.

22. Suppose aliens abducted you as you were walking to school. Write a letter to your best friend on Earth telling him or her about this experience.

23. Imagine yourself as a passenger on a bus. The bus driver announces, "We're here! Everyone off." As the bus pulls away, you realize you don't know where you are. Describe to your family the surroundings in which you find yourself and the adventure you have trying to get home.

24. You have enrolled as a freshman in college, but you are only 10 years old. Write a story to a friend telling about a day at college. Be sure to describe the atmosphere and tell what impressed you most about your experience.

25. To tell a story, we often take photographs or create paintings. Imagine yourself dropped into the scene represented by a painting, photograph, or image. Write a story for a younger student that stars you as a character in the painting, photograph, or image. (*Note to teacher:* Prepare to have a painting, photograph, or image on hand, such as a famous painting, a postcard, or a vacation brochure.)

26. Picture yourself awakened as an animal, an object, or a gas. Write a story to tell a human friend what your new life is like.

27. Imagine you are a newspaper reporter covering the Revolutionary War. You find yourself pinned down by a wave of enemy troops. Write a newspaper story telling readers what your experience is like.

28. Suppose you woke up one morning to find that everyone had disappeared, there was no electricity, telephones had stopped working, and the world had run out of gasoline. Write an account for future generations of what life was like with this sudden change.

29. During a hiking trip, you find yourself lost in the woods. It is getting dark, and you are afraid. Suddenly you are saved—by the Three Bears. Where do they take you? What is it like in their house?

30. A travel agency is looking for exciting vacation destinations that are a bit out of the ordinary. Imagine that the agency asks you to explore the islands of the Caribbean on a magic carpet. Write an account for them to describe the interesting experiences you have there.

31. Imagine that as you are taking a shortcut through the woods, a tree topples, pinning you underneath. With only a few branches and an old rope conveniently left nearby, explain for your science teacher how you freed yourself.

32. Imagine that you find a page torn from a short story that has only two lines: "That's how I became known as 'Captain.' THE END." For a friend, create another story that could have this exact ending.

Descriptive Narrative Prompts

Descriptive prompts are helpful in giving students ideas on subjects about which they can write descriptively. Here are seventy possible themes for descriptive prompts. The corresponding prompts follow.

Themes
1. An annoying sound
2. Your favorite outdoor activity
3. Your least favorite vegetable
4. Meeting a famous person
5. Your favorite smell
6. Your favorite store
7. Your favorite season
8. The best dream you ever had
9. The best ice cream sundae
10. Your favorite book
11. Your favorite day
12. A spring shower
13. Your favorite body of water
14. A sunset
15. Your favorite fast food
16. A bad day
17. Your room
18. Your favorite sport
19. A family member
20. Your favorite after-school activity
21. Outdoors in the wintertime
22. Your favorite zoo animal
23. Your favorite teacher
24. A flower
25. Your favorite holiday

26. Your favorite toy
27. Your favorite Halloween costume
28. The best day of your life
29. Your classroom
30. Your favorite room in the house
31. Your favorite piece of jewelry
32. Your favorite pair of shoes
33. Your favorite vehicle
34. A hat
35. The front of your home
36. The circus
37. Perfect weather
38. Your breakfast table today
39. A visit to the dentist
40. Your favorite Christmas ornament
41. The most interesting present you have received
42. What you think is at the end of the rainbow
43. Teacher for a day
44. How a flower feels during a storm
45. You are an insect
46. Strangest dream you remember
47. A character from a book
48. Walking on the moon
49. Your favorite outfit
50. Your "happy place"
51. The scariest thing that ever happened to you
52. Your backyard
53. The ocean
54. Your favorite person
55. Sounds in your neighborhood during the day
56. Sounds at the zoo
57. Your favorite cartoon character
58. Your favorite soda
59. Your favorite chair
60. A clock (analog)
61. The personality of your favorite color
62. Your bedspread

63. A dream catcher

64. Your favorite candy bar

65. The supermarket

66. Your neighborhood at night

67. Your favorite stuffed animal

68. Your favorite book bag

69. A new hair style

70. Your favorite pizza

Descriptive Narrative Prompts

1. Describe the most annoying sound that you have ever heard. Tell what or who made the sound, why, and how.

2. Choose one of your favorite outdoor activities and describe it so that a listener could take part in the activity by following your description.

3. Choose your least favorite vegetable. Describe how it looks, smells, and tastes.

4. If you could meet any famous person, whom would you choose and why? Describe to the reader where you would choose to meet and what questions you would ask the person.

5. Describe your favorite smell so that anyone who reads your paper can imagine that scent.

6. Choose your favorite store and describe where it is, what it looks like, and what it sells.

7. Describe your favorite season so that anyone reading your paper would know which of the seasons you are talking about.

8. Describe the best dream you have ever had. Who was in it, where were you, and what were you doing?

9. Describe the best ice cream sundae that could ever be made. Include what it would look like and what would be on it.

10. Choose your favorite book and describe how it makes you feel to read it.

11. Think of your favorite day. Describe its sights, sounds, and colors so that anyone who reads your paper will feel like he or she is there.

12. Describe a spring shower, how it looks, feels, and smells so that anyone who reads your paper will feel like he or she just walked in out of the rain.

13. Choose your favorite body of water (for example, a lake, river, or stream) and describe it.

14. Describe a sunset so that colors will jump off the paper and anyone who reads the paper can imagine it.

15. What is your favorite type of fast food, and how do you like to eat it? Describe this so that the reader's mouth will water.

16. Everyone has bad days. Describe one of your bad days so that the reader will vividly understand what happened.

17. Describe your room and how it looked when you left home this morning.

18. Describe your favorite sport. The catch is that you cannot use the name of the sport in your paper. The reader must be able to identify the sport from your description.

19. Describe a member of your family so that if your friend came to your family reunion he or she could pick this family member out of the crowd.

20. Describe your favorite after-school activity.

21. Describe what the outdoors looks like at your home during the winter season.

22. Describe your favorite zoo animal.

23. Describe your favorite teacher. Tell how he or she looks and acts.

24. Choose a flower and describe how it smells and looks.

25. Describe your favorite holiday of the year.

26. Describe your favorite toy.

27. Describe your favorite Halloween costume.

28. Think of a time when you felt it was the best day of your life and describe it. How did it feel? What happened?

29. Describe your classroom. Tell how it looks so that someone visiting your school could pick it out of all the rooms in the school.

30. Describe your favorite room in your house.

31. Describe your favorite piece of jewelry.

32. Describe your favorite pair of shoes.

33. Choose a vehicle that you like. Describe how it looks.

34. Describe a hat that you own or you have seen. Tell how it looks.

35. Describe the front of your home. Tell how it looks so that anyone could find it strictly from your description.

36. Imagine you are at the circus. Describe what you see there.

37. Describe the weather on a perfect summer day. This should be the day that you think is perfect for summer, not that anyone else might call perfect.

38. Describe the scene at your breakfast table this morning so that the reader can picture it.

39. Describe your most recent visit to the dentist.

40. Describe your favorite ornament that is put on your Christmas tree each year.

41. Describe the most interesting present that you have ever received.

42. Describe what you think might be at the end of the rainbow.

43. Imagine you are a teacher. Describe what you would do in the classroom for a day.

44. Describe how a flower might feel during a storm.

45. Pretend you are an insect. Describe yourself so that others will be able to tell what insect you are.

46. Describe the strangest dream you can remember. Describe the sequence of events and what you felt during your dream so that the reader feels like a part of the dream.

47. Describe a character in a book that you have read recently. Describe the character's weakness and virtues and his or her joys and sorrows. Describe the person's physical demeanor also.

48. You have been chosen by NASA to be the first student to travel to the moon. Describe your experience while you were walking around on the moon.

49. Describe your favorite outfit so that the reader could go into your closet and pull it out.

50. Describe the place you go when you need to relax and get away from all of life's troubles.

51. Describe the scariest event that has ever occurred in your life. Describe the emotions you felt before, during, and after the event took place.

52. Describe your backyard. Describe your lawn furniture and the other objects that are visible in your backyard. Describe it as if you are looking out your back door.

53. Describe the ocean so that anyone who has never seen it before can see how it looks, how it smells, and how it tastes.

54. Think of your favorite person and describe him or her so that he or she could be picked out of a crowd.

55. Describe the sounds you hear in your neighborhood during the daytime.

56. Describe the sounds you would hear while visiting the zoo.

57. Think of your favorite cartoon character. Tell how he or she looks so that someone reading your paper could guess who it is.

58. Think of your (least?) favorite soda and describe how it smells, tastes, and looks.

59. Describe your favorite chair. How does it look, and how does it feel when you sit in it?

60. Describe what an analog clock looks like. This is the familiar clock with hands, not a digital one.

61. Colors seem to have a personality. Describe the personality of your favorite color.

62. Describe the bedspread on your bed. How does it look, feel, and smell?

63. Describe what a dream catcher looks like so the reader can visualize what it looks like.

64. Think of your favorite candy bar. Describe the candy as well as its wrapper.

65. Describe the sights and sounds of your last visit to the supermarket.

66. Describe what someone might hear and see in your neighborhood late at night.

67. Describe your favorite stuffed animal so that someone reading your paper could recognize it.

68. Describe your favorite book bag so it could be found if it were lost.

69. Describe a new hair style that you might consider trying.

70. Which type of pizza is your favorite? Describe how it looks, smells, and tastes.

GLOSSARY

Alliteration: A poetic effect achieved by using several words that begin with the same letter or similar sound, as in "Peter Piper picked a peck of pickled peppers."

Autobiographical: A self-descriptive narrative in which the writer writes about him- or herself.

Ballad: A poem, usually related in a traditional style, telling a story in a number of short regular stanzas, often with a refrain.

Biographical Sketch: A short, written account that describes a famous person.

Brainstorming: A process of generating ideas spontaneously, especially in a focused group discussion, where ideas are not rejected because of analysis.

Cadence: The manner in which poetry flows according to a rhythm.

Character Sketch: A short, written account that describes the personal attributes of a person or a personalized animal.

Characterization: The way in which a writer portrays the characters in a narrative writing.

Climax: The most important or exciting point in a story.

Dialogue: A work, or a section of a literary work, that contains a preponderance of spoken words exchanged between characters.

Diamonte: A seven-line poem on two contrasting topics, with strict word usage and line length requirements, so that the poem visually resembles a diamond.

Fable: A short story with a moral, especially one in which the characters are animals.

Fairy Tale: A short story with love and/or adventure included in the plot. It usually includes a magical event as a key element of the story.

Genre: The categories that artistic works are divided into on the basis of form, style, or subject matter.

Haiku: Poetry with seventeen syllables, organized in three lines of five, seven, and five syllables, usually describing nature.

Hyperbole: Obvious exaggeration used for effect.

Limerick: A five-line humorous poem with regular meter and rhyme patterns.

Moral: A conclusion drawn from a story about how to behave or proceed ethically.

Onomatopoeia: Words that imitate the sound associated with the thing or action in question, such as "hiss" and "whack."

Quatrain: A verse of poetry consisting of four lines.

Refrain: A group of lines that recurs at regular intervals in a poem.

Stanza: Lines of verse forming a separate unit within a poem.

Syllabic: Pertaining to syllables, as in syllabic cadence.

Tall Tale: A narrative that exaggerates something beyond the bounds of probability.

BIBLIOGRAPHY

Aragon, Jane Chelsea. *Salt Hands*. Illustrated by Ted Rand. New York: Dutton, 1989.

Atwell, Nancie. *In the Middle: Writing, Reading, and Learning with Adolescents*. Portsmouth, N.H.: Boynton/Cook-Heinemann, 1987.

Banks, Lynne Reid. *The Indian in the Cupboard*. New York: Avon Books, 1980.

Barth, Roland. *Improving Schools from Within: Teachers, Parents, and Principal Can Make the Difference*. San Francisco: Jossey-Bass, 1990.

Barth, Roland S. *Run School Run*. Cambridge, Mass.: Harvard University Press, 1980.

Batzle, Janine. *Portfolio Assessment and Evaluation*. Cypress, Calif.: Creative Teaching Press, 1992.

Baylor, Byrd. *Everybody Needs a Rock*. Pictures by Peter Pamall. New York: Aladdin Books, 1974.

Baylor, Byrd. *The Other Way to Listen*. New York: Charles Scribner's Sons, 1978.

Baylor, Byrd. *The Best Town in the World*. Pictures by Ronald Himier. New York: Macmillan, 1982.

Baylor, Byrd, and Peter Pamall. *Your Own Best Secret Place*. New York: Charles Scribner's Sons, 1979.

Bissex, Glenda. *GNYS AT WRK: A Child Learns to Write and Read*. Cambridge, Mass.: Harvard University Press, 1980.

Blos, Joan, and Stephen Yammell. *Old Henry*. New York: Mulberry Books, 1987.

Brinckloe, Julie. *Fireflies*. New York: Macmillan, 1985.

Bunting, Eve. *The Wednesday Surprise*. Illustrated by Donald Carrick. New York: Clarion Books, 1989.

Cisneros, Sandra. *The House on Mango Street*. New York: Vintage Books, 1989.

Collins, Pat Lowery. *I Am an Artist*. Illustrated by Robin Brickman. Brookfield, Conn.: Milbrook Press, 1992.

DeFelice, Cynthia. *When Grampa Kissed His Elbow*. Illustrated by Karl Swanson. New York: Macmillan, 1992.

Elbow, Peter. *Writing with Power: Techniques for Mastering the Writing Process*. New York: Oxford University Press, 1981.

Fletcher, Ralph. *What a Writer Needs*. Portsmouth, N.H.: Heinemann, 1992.

Flynn, Kris. *Graphic Organizers*. Cypress, Calif.: Creative Teaching Press, 1995.

Fox, Paula. *Monkey Island*. New York: Orchard Books, 1991.

Gardiner, John Reynolds. *Stone Fox*. New York: Crowell, 1980.

Gardner, Howard. *Artful Scribbles: The Significance of Children's Drawings*. New York: Basic Books, 1980.

Goodman, Ken. *What's Whole in Whole Language?* Portsmouth, N.H.: Heinemann, 1986.

Graves, Donald H. *Writing: Teachers and Children at Work*. Portsmouth, N.H.: Heinemann, 1983.

Graves, Donald H. *A Fresh Look at Writing*. Portsmouth, N.H.: Heinemann, 1994.

Graves, Donald H., and Bonnie S. Sunstein. *Portfolio Portraits*. Portsmouth, N.H.: Heinemann, 1992.

Greenfield, Eloise. *First Pink Light*. Illustrated by Jan Spivey Gilchrist. New York: Black Butterfly Children's Books, 1976.

Grover, Mary, and Linda Sheppard. *Not on Your Own: The Power of Learning Together*. Toronto: Scholastic, 1989.

Hale, Nancy. *The Realities of Fiction*. Boston: Little, Brown, 1961.

Harste, Jerome C., Virginia A. Woodward, and Carolyn L. Burke. *Language Stories and Literacy Lessons*. Portsmouth, N.H.: Heinemann, 1984.

Harwayne, Shelley. *Lasting Impressions: Weaving Literature into the Writing Workshop*. Portsmouth, N.H.: Heinemann, 1992.

Heard, Georgia. *For the Good of the Earth and Sun: Teaching Poetry*. Portsmouth, N.H.: Heinemann, 1989.

Heide, Florence Parry, and Judith Heide Gillitan. *The Day of Ahmed's Secret*. Illustrated by Ted Lewin. New York: Lothrop, Lee and Shepard, 1990.

Hoffman, Mary. *Amazing Grace*. Pictures by Caroline Binch. New York: Dial Books, 1991.

Isadora, Katherine. *Ben's Trumpet*. New York: Mulberry Books, 1979.

Jaggar, Angela, and M. Trika Smith-Burke (Eds.). *Observing the Language Learner*. Newark, Del.: International Reading Association; Urbana, IL: National Council of Teachers of English, 1985.

Janeczko, Paul B. *The Place My Words Are Looking For*. New York: Macmillan Children's Book Group, 1990.

Lowry, Lois. *Autumn Street*. New York: Dell, 1980.

Lowry, Lois. *Number the Stars*. New York: Dell, 1989.

MacLachlan, Patricia. *Through Grandpa's Eyes*. Illustrated by Deborah Kogan Ray. New York: HarperCollins, 1980.

Mathers, Petra. *Sophie and Lou*. New York: HarperCollins Children's Books, 1991.

Mayher, John. *Uncommon Sense: Theoretical Practice in Language Education*. Portsmouth, N.H.: Boynton/Cook-Heinemann, 1990.

McCarthy, Tara. *150 Thematic Writing Activities*. New York: Scholastic, 1993.

McLerran, Alice. *Roxaboxen*. Illustrated by Barbara Cooney. New York: Lothrop, Lee and Shepard, 1990.

McNulty, Faith. *The Lady and the Spider.* Illustrated by Steve Marstall. New York: HarperCollins Children's Books, 1987.

Murray, Donald M. *Learning by Teaching: Selected Articles on Uniting and Teaching.* Portsmouth, N.H.: Boynton/Cook-Heinemann, 1982.

Murray, Donald M. *Write to Learn.* New York: Holt, 1984.

Murray, Donald M. *A Writer Teaches Writing* (2nd ed.). Boston: Houghton Mifflin, 1985.

Murray, Donald M. *Expecting the Unexpected: Teaching Myself and Others to Read and Write.* Portsmouth, N.H.: Boynton/Cook-Heinemann, 1989.

Myers, Walter Dean. *Scorpions.* New York: HarperCollins, 1988.

Newkirk, Thomas. *More Than Stories: The Range of Children's Writing.* Portsmouth, N.H.: Heinemann, 1989.

Paterson, Katherine. *Lyddie.* New York: Lodestar Books, 1991.

Paulsen, Gary. *The Monument.* New York: Delacorte Press, 1991.

Perl, Sondra, and Nancy Wilson. *Through Teachers' Eyes: Portraits of Writing Teachers at Work.* Portsmouth, N.H.: Heinemann, 1986.

Peterson, Ralph. *Life in a Crowded Place: Making a Learning Community.* Portsmouth, N.H.: Heinemann, 1992.

Reid, Margarette S. *The Button Box.* Illustrated by Sarah Chamberlain. New York: Dutton Children's Books, 1990.

Routman, Regie. *Transitions: From Literature to Literacy.* Portsmouth, N.H.: Heinemann, 1988.

Shaughnessy, Mina. *Errors and Expectations.* New York: Oxford University Press, 1977.

Short, Kathy G., and Carolyn Burke. *Creating Curriculum: Teachers and Students as a Community of Learners.* Portsmouth, N.H.: Heinemann, 1991.

Smith, Doris Buchanan. *A Taste of Blackberries.* New York: Thomas Y. Crowell, 1973.

Smith, Frank. *Insult to Intelligence: The Bureaucratic Invasion of Our Classrooms.* Portsmouth, N.H.: Heinemann, 1986.

Sparks, J. E. *Write for Power.* Los Angeles: Communication Associates, 1995.

Spinelli, Jerry. *Maniac Magee.* Boston: Little, Brown, 1990.

Steiner, Vera John (Ed.). *Notebooks of the Mind.* Albuquerque: University of New Mexico Press, 1985.

Temple, Charles A., Ruth O. Nathan, and Nancy A. Burnig. *The Beginnings of Writing.* Needham Heights, Mass.: Allyn and Bacon, 1982.

Van Manen, Max. *The Tone of Teaching.* Portsmouth, N.H.: Heinemann, 1986.

Wilde, Sandra. *You Kan Red This!* *Spelling and Punctuation for Whole Language Classrooms, K–6.* Portsmouth, N.H.: Heinemann, 1991.

Yashima, Taro. *Crow Boy.* New York: Puffin Books, 1976.

Zinsser, William (Ed.). *Inventing the Truth: The Art and Craft of Memoir.* Boston: Houghton Mifflin, 1987.

Zinsser, William. *On Writing Well.* New York: HarperCollins, 1990.